The Miser

by Freyda Thomas

Inspired by Molière's *L'Avare*

A SAMUEL FRENCH ACTING EDITION

SAMUELFRENCH.COM

Copyright © 2012 by Freyda Thomas

ALL RIGHTS RESERVED

Cover art by Joshua Friedman

\CAUTION: Professionals and amateurs are hereby warned that *THE MISER* is subject to a licensing fee. It is fully protected under the copyright laws of the United States of America, the British Commonwealth, including Canada, and all other countries of the Copyright Union. All rights, including professional, amateur, motion picture, recitation, lecturing, public reading, radio broadcasting, television and the rights of translation into foreign languages are strictly reserved. In its present form the play is dedicated to the reading public only.

The amateur and professional live stage performance rights to *THE MISER* are controlled exclusively by Samuel French, Inc., and licensing arrangements and performance licenses must be secured well in advance of presentation. PLEASE NOTE that amateur licensing fees are set upon application in accordance with your producing circumstances. When applying for a licensing quotation and a performance license please give us the number of performances intended, dates of production, your seating capacity and admission fee. Licensing fees are payable one week before the opening performance of the play to Samuel French, Inc., at 45 W. 25th Street, New York, NY 10010.

Licensing fee of the required amount must be paid whether the play is presented for charity or gain and whether or not admission is charged.

Professional/Stock licensing fees quoted upon application to Samuel French, Inc.

For all other rights than those stipulated above, apply to: Harden-Curtis Associates, 850 Seventh Avenue, Suite 903, New York, NY 10019; attn: Mary Harden

Particular emphasis is laid on the question of amateur or professional readings, permission and terms for which must be secured in writing from Samuel French, Inc.

Copying from this book in whole or in part is strictly forbidden by law, and the right of performance is not transferable.

Whenever the play is produced the following notice must appear on all programs, printing and advertising for the play: "Produced by special arrangement with Samuel French, Inc."

Due authorship credit must be given on all programs, printing and advertising for the play.

ISBN 978-0-573-70030-9   Printed in U.S.A.   #20259

No one shall commit or authorize any act or omission by which the copyright of, or the right to copyright, this play may be impaired.

No one shall make any changes in this play for the purpose of production.

Publication of this play does not imply availability for performance. Both amateurs and professionals considering a production are strongly advised in their own interests to apply to Samuel French, Inc., for written permission before starting rehearsals, advertising, or booking a theatre.

No part of this book may be reproduced, stored in a retrieval system, or transmitted in any form, by any means, now known or yet to be invented, including mechanical, electronic, photocopying, recording, videotaping, or otherwise, without the prior written permission of the publisher.

MUSIC USE NOTE

Licensees are solely responsible for obtaining formal written permission from copyright owners to use copyrighted music in the performance of this play and are strongly cautioned to do so. If no such permission is obtained by the licensee, then the licensee must use only original music that the licensee owns and controls. Licensees are solely responsible and liable for all music clearances and shall indemnify the copyright owners of the play and their licensing agent, Samuel French, Inc., against any costs, expenses, losses and liabilities arising from the use of music by licensees.

IMPORTANT BILLING AND CREDIT REQUIREMENTS

All producers of *THE MISER* must give credit to the Author of the Play in all programs distributed in connection with performances of the Play, and in all instances in which the title of the Play appears for the purposes of advertising, publicizing or otherwise exploiting the Play and/or a production. The name of the Author *must* appear on a separate line on which no other name appears, immediately following the title and *must* appear in size of type not less than fifty percent of the size of the title type.

CHARACTERS

HARPAGON - 60s, a miser

ELISE - early 20s, his daughter

VALERE - valet to Harpagon, in love with Elise

CLEANTE - son to Harpagon, in love with Marianne

MARIANNE - 18, the girl next door

LA FLECHE - 20s, 30s, valet to Cleante, disguises himself as a German marriage contractor

MAITRE JACQUES - young to middle-age, Ze chef

FROSINE - 40ish, a marriage broker, disguises herself as the lisping Mme. Poquelin

MAITRE SIMON - young to middle-age, a broker, also plays Inspector Sansclou

INSPECTOR SANSCLOU - the original Clouseau, played by the Actor playing Simon

SEÑOR ANSELME - the Deus ex Machina, 50s, father to both Marianne and Valere

For Eyanna and Angelina
My nieces and the light in my life

ACT ONE

(The shabby salon of **HARPAGON**. *Sparsely furnished. One entrance stage right to the front door, one entrance stage left to the kitchen and other parts of the house. Entrance to the garden upstage center with large glass windows and a door. One old sofa with a pillow on it in the salon. Discoloration on the walls where paintings once hung.* **HARPAGON** *is discovered, downstage left, alone, sitting at a writing desk, with quill pen, paper, and piles of coins. He is doing the bills. He speaks alone.)*

HARPAGON. Fifteen sous for the horses! The horses!? Animals!? What are they eating!? Golden oats!? Ridiculous. Six, and not a penny more.

(He counts out a few coins.)

Wages, the cook. Why do we need a cook? My daughter, my son, my house-man, my cook–All these people underfoot, depending on me for their livelihood! Costing money every time they lift a spoon. They're going to break me, all of them! Especially my ungrateful, spoiled children who want things, things, things! And I'm the supplier. We won't make it through the day with these bills. *(looking through list)* Shoes resoled? Oh, yes, mine.

(He counts out the coins and places them with the others.)

My son would just go and buy a new pair. My son has to have a valet! He can't put on his own clothes!?

(He checks off the list.)

Well, that's it. And we've got some left over. But it's never enough. Precious little. God knows we're going to need it. But it's not enough! I've got to make more.

HARPAGON. *(cont.)* How can I make more? Who makes more out there? Who always has enough money? Hah! The money lenders—the blood-sucking money lenders! If I want to have enough, I have to become one of them! It's as simple as that. I've got to find someone to help me get a money-lending business going. Who do I know? Hah! Send someone to fetch him. Valere! Valere!

(no response)

Where can he be off to? Where is everybody when I need them! La Fleche!? LA FLECHE!!?? I told my son that valet of his was a good-for-nothing, but did he listen!? Jacques! Jacques!!??

(**JACQUES** *comes bolting into the room, apron on, slapping his chef's hat on.*)

MAITRE JACQUES. Oui, monsieur! Shall I prepare a dinner!?

HARPAGON. No, no no. I want you to go on an errand.

MAITRE JACQUES. Oh, for some cutlets? Some fromage? Shall I bring 'ome somesing speciale for tonight?

HARPAGON. No, no no! Your vegetable soup is perfectly fine.

MAITRE JACQUES. Oui, monsieur. But I make eet every night.

HARPAGON. And you'll go on making it every night, as long as we have vegetables from the garden. Gardens are thrifty.

MAITRE JACQUES. Oui, monsieur.

HARPAGON. Here, take this note to the market. Look for a man.

MAITRE JACQUES. Oui monsieur. *(He starts to go, then stops.)* Could you be a beet more specifique?

HARPAGON. He looks foreign.

MAITRE JACQUES. Foreign. From where?

HARPAGON. I don't know! He's very strangely dressed. He was pointed out to me last week.

MAITRE JACQUES. Ah, oui.

(He looks to the audience for help.)

HARPAGON. And don't come back without an answer.

MAITRE JACQUES. Oui, monsieur. *(He starts to go, dejected.)* Are you sure you don't want—

HARPAGON. I'M SURE!

*(**MAITRE JACQUES** goes. **HARPAGON** puts his coins into a cashbox, locks it, puts the key in his pocket, looks around the room, starts for the garden, then hears the offstage voices of **ELISE** and **VALERE**)*

STAY OUT! OUT!

(The voices stop abruptly.)

Can't let them see the cashbox. Can't let anyone know where I hide it. They'd rob me blind. DON'T ANYONE COME IN HERE, DO YOU HEAR ME! Not to worry, nobody will find it where I've buried it. Who would think of looking in the garden!? That's right—grow your own vegetables, it's much cheaper. And they grow so much faster and larger with gold under them!

*(He exits upstage center into the garden, which can only partially be seen from the audience. **LA FLECHE** enters from behind the screen.)*

LA FLECHE. Screens are very useful things. You can learn so much. I think I'll hold on to that information for a while. I have a feeling it will come in handy.

*(He exits. A pause, then enter **ELISE** and **VALERE**. **ELISE** is carrying a basket of clothes, **VALERE** has a dustpan and broom. They look around the room, see no one, drop their items and rush into each other's arms. as they speak their opening lines.)*

VALERE. I love you.

ELISE. I love *you.*

VALERE. I love you more.

ELISE. Impossible.

VALERE. Very possible...

(another kiss)

ELISE. Oh but, dearest, I can't help worrying about how all of this is going to turn out.

VALERE. You know, you're a lot like your father, sometimes.

ELISE. I am not!

VALERE. You're both worrywarts. He just worries about money.

ELISE. Well, so do I! How can we marry without it? And where can we get some? And will you still love me if it takes us ten years, or worse, if we have to wait for him to die!?

VALERE. He'll never die. He's too cheap to pay for a funeral.

ELISE. Don't joke.

VALERE. All right, no jokes. How about kisses?

(They approach for another go, and–)

HARPAGON. *(from the garden)* Ungrateful brats! Children! A waste of time and money. Bloodsuckers!

*(***ELISE** *and* **VALERE** *break their embrace and turn from each other.* **HARPAGON** *re-enters from the garden and speaks to* **ELISE.***)*

Well? Did you finish the mending? Make the beds? Dust? Have you finished your chores?

ELISE. Almost, father.

HARPAGON. Hah! Slacker! *(to* **VALERE***)* Valere! Did you sweep the stairs?

VALERE. I have, sir.

HARPAGON. You should have been my son, instead of that ungrateful money-grubbing lout I spawned. *(to* **ELISE***)* Your brother is a leech, and you're no better!

VALERE. I'm sure both your children love and respect you, sir.

HARPAGON. Hah! Always asking for things, things, things! Why does a girl need more than one dress? Why does a young man need a horse? He should walk, get exercise. Exercise keeps you trim. Then you don't need as much food. It's hard enough feeding everyone in this house on one little garden.

ELISE. It seems to be doing very well, father.

HARPAGON. *(terrified)* The garden!? Why, yes. I was just checking on the progress. Making sure no worms are eating our food. That's all we've got, you know.

ELISE. So you've said.

VALERE. I'll be happy to pull the worms off the plants, sir, in my spare time.

HARPAGON. NO! I mean, it's a sensitive garden. Everything wilts if a stranger goes in. It likes me—only me. Stay out of the garden or we'll all starve. Both of you. Everybody. Do you hear me!? OUT!

(He exits, growling and grumbling.)

ELISE. I have to admit that I wish sometimes that my father was...someone else.

VALERE. Who?

ELISE. Anyone else.

VALERE. You must be patient a little longer, my love. It will work out. You have to learn how to...play him, like a harpsichord. Strike the right note and make a beautiful melody. We'll find a way to make an entire symphony together. Love always triumphs.

ELISE. I'm so afraid you'll give up on me and leave. I don't know why you've bothered hanging around here so many weeks. It's so...gloomy.

VALERE. Not when I look at you.

ELISE. You don't look at me. Men only look at you when they want you.

VALERE. And I want you all the time. I just can't...look when your father is around. You don't want him to guess, do you? And he's around, you notice. All the time.

ELISE. I know. He's so irascible and crabby. He wasn't always like this. He used to be...almost generous. It's just since this...

BOTH. Economic downturn.

ELISE. What can we do? We can't afford to run away. He doesn't even pay you a salary!

VALERE. I know.

ELISE. I don't know why you stay. You should leave me and go search for your poor lost family.

VALERE. You know why I stay.

(They kiss. **HARPAGON** *re-enters, crossing and mumbling.* **ELISE** *and* **VALERE** *break the kiss.* **ELISE** *picks up a garment and pretends to sew.* **VALERE** *grabs the dustpan and broom and sweeps.)*

HARPAGON. Ugh, this economy. It's killing me!

(He exits to the other side. **ELISE** *and* **VALERE** *go back to kissing.)*

ELISE. I'm so…FRUSTRATED!

VALERE. You are!? I've wanted to marry you ever since the first moment I laid eyes on you.

ELISE. Under water?

VALERE. Under water, hair all billowed out—you looked like a mermaid.

ELISE. A drowning mermaid. And you saved my life. I'll never forget that horrible shipwreck.

VALERE. I loved that shipwreck. It brought you to me.

ELISE. Oh, I want to shout to the world, "Look at this wonderful man who loves me!"

VALERE. Not yet, my darling. Your father would throw me into the street, and then we wouldn't see each other every day. Not yet.

(They kiss again, then break quickly when they hear **HARPAGON** *with* **LA FLECHE** *offstage.* **HARPAGON** *and* **LA FLECHE** *enter, cross, and exit to the other side.)*

HARPAGON. I called you before and you didn't answer! Probably off stealing something of mine. You're nothing but a common thief! Out of my house!

LA FLECHE. What!? What did I steal!?

HARPAGON. I don't know! When I catch you, I'll find out what!

LA FLECHE. I swear on my mother's grave—

HARPAGON. Your mother's alive!

LA FLECHE. When she finds out you called me a thief, it'll kill her.

(They exit, running. **ELISE** *and* **VALERE** *go back to their embrace.)*

ELISE. How long can we go on like this!? Oh, why won't my father give me my pitiful little inheritance from my mother? We could run away together.

VALERE. A little patience, my love. It will all work out. Meanwhile I'll continue to play up to your father, keep him as calm as possible, and we'll have our stolen moments.

ELISE. I don't know how you tolerate him. I always lose my temper.

VALERE. I know you do, and it only makes him worse! You have to learn how to make it a kind of game. Today I gave him six compliments and I got him where I wanted him. Yesterday I had to give him eight. It's almost mathematical. How strongly do I play upon his fears until he gives in? And make no mistake, that man is riddled with fear. When I get a little tired, a little bored with the ridiculousness of it all, I look at you. That's the trick. Keep your eye on the prize.

ELISE. How do you know you'll win it?

VALERE. I'd say I already have. Just the delivery is missing.

ELISE. Yes, one small delivery. And the money.

(They share another kiss. **ELISE** *breaks it.)*

ELISE. My brother!

VALERE. Cléante? What about him?

ELISE. He has a little money. Father had to give him his part of mother's inheritance—he had to, Cléante is older. And a man. He might lend us enough to get away!

VALERE. I don't want to take money I'm not sure I can pay back. Who knows if I'll find my relatives? I lost them so long ago, they may not be alive any longer.

ELISE. You must find them. I know Cléante will help us.

CLEANTE. *(entering, jubilant and well-dressed)* Did someone mention my name?

ELISE. Cléante! You look so…nice.

CLEANTE. I know! I spent practically my last sous on this. And some other things.

ELISE. You're out of money!?

CLEANTE. Just about.

VALERE. So much for that idea.

ELISE. Why did you spend all your money on clothes!?

CLEANTE. Because clothes make the man, and this man is…in love!

ELISE. You're in love?

VALERE. He's in love.

CLEANTE. I'm in love.

ELISE. You weren't in love yesterday.

CLEANTE. Well, I am today!

ELISE. That's impossible! You can't fall in love so quickly.

VALERE. Can't you?

CLEANTE. You've never been in love. You couldn't know how it is.

VALERE. *(interrupting **ELISE**, who is about to refute that statement)* You're right—she couldn't know.

ELISE. Well, who is she?

CLEANTE. Who is she? Who is she? Just the sweetest, dearest, kindest, most beautiful creature anyone has ever laid eyes on.

ELISE. And her name is…

CLEANTE. Marianne. *(singing)* Marianne, Marianne, oh my dear Marianne…

VALERE. Nice name.

ELISE. How did you meet?

CLEANTE. *(still singing)* How did we meet? How did we meet? Why, down the street, down this very street!

VALERE. He really is in love, isn't he?

ELISE. It would appear so.

CLEANTE. She lives right down the street. Just moved in, with her poor, frail, invalid mother.

ELISE & VALERE. *(all sympathy)* Ohh.

CLEANTE. Oh, you should see the way Marianne takes care of her—caters to her, tends to her every little need. No mother could ask for a better daughter.

VALERE. And no man could ask for a better wife?

CLEANTE. Yes, exactly!

ELISE. And have you informed our father of this…event?

CLEANTE. Oh, father. You would go and spoil it. He won't like her.

VALERE. Why not?

CLEANTE. They're not exactly rich.

VALERE. Not exactly rich. How not exactly rich are they?

CLEANTE. Poor.

ELISE. Ah, just like us.

CLEANTE. Us!? If we knew where father was hiding his fortune, we'd all be set for life. I could get married, La Fleche could get a raise, you could get a new gown and find a husband!

VALERE. Imagine that. You think he has money hidden somewhere around here?

CLEANTE. I'm sure of it. He sold off all his assets a while back. I heard him. The walls have ears.

VALERE. And not much else.

CLEANTE. He doesn't trust the banks or the investment houses any more. I think he's turned everything into gold! And I'm going to find out where it is.

ELISE. Well, I hope you're in a sharing mood when you do.

CLEANTE. Don't you worry. He has just so over-reacted to this… what-would-you-call-it…crunch the country is in. It will pass, it always does. You have to keep a positive attitude.

ELISE. When have you ever seen him with a positive attitude?

CLEANTE. Once, when I was very little. Well, I have a positive attitude, why can't he?

ELISE. I think you got that from mother.

CLEANTE. Oh, if only mother could have met Marianne. I'm sure she would have approved. If only I could bring her here, invite her over, but how could I invite anyone to this…disgusting hovel? He sold all the furniture, the paintings, and the rugs to buy gold. It used to look so elegant!

ELISE. Well, it's clean, I can guarantee you that.

VALERE. He must be hoarding the gold somewhere in the house.

CLEANTE. I've looked high and low, in the middle of the night, when he's asleep. Meanwhile, I have a plan to borrow some money to, well, fix up the place for an afternoon, so I can invite my dear, sweet Marianne to come over. Perhaps throw a dinner party! A nice, juicy boeuf bourguignon, escargots, Crème Chantilly,…

VALERE. I hope she's a vegetarian. The only meal you'll get out of him will be from the garden. Have you seen his horses? He doesn't even feed them. You could play a minuet on their ribs with a stick.

CLEANTE. It's so unfair!

*(***HARPAGON***'s voice, offstage)*

Here he comes! I'm going out to find my valet. I sent him to find a money lender who can arrange everything! Dinner tonight at eight!

VALERE. And we have chores to finish!

(They exit as **LA FLECHE** *enters, being chased by* **HARPAGON**.*)*

HARPAGON. GET OUT!

*(***LA FLECHE** *starts to go.)*

STOP!

LA FLECHE. *(stopping)* Which is it?

HARPAGON. I want you out of my house. But I want to make sure you're not taking anything with you. Come over here.

(LA FLECHE slowly starts toward HARPAGON, speaks aside.)

LA FLECHE. *(aside, to audience)* I don't think I'm going to like this. You know, I'd rather just leave, but I can't. There's no work out there! And his son is paying me, so I have to put up with his…his…well, you see what he's like.

(He stands before HARPAGON.)

HARPAGON. *(pointing to his breeches)* What have you got in there?

LA FLECHE. What have I got!? The same as any man. Maybe a little more.

HARPAGON. Aha!

(HARPAGON starts to stick his hand in LA FLECHE's breeches. LA FLECHE pulls away.)

LA FLECHE. Hey hey hey! I don't think so.

HARPAGON. You're hiding something, I know it!

LA FLECHE. I'm hiding what everybody hides! And you're not going in there!

HARPAGON. Empty your pockets, then, all of them.

(LA FLECHE starts emptying a host of different pockets: bits of string, buttons, strange looking tools, toys, a very long scarf, etc, which he dumps into HARPAGON's hands.)

LA FLECHE. There. There's your fortune. Spend it wisely.

HARPAGON. *(mumbling to himself)* He thinks he's outsmarted me, but he hasn't.

LA FLECHE. Talking to himself? Not a good sign. Clearly the man is a lunatic.

HARPAGON. Who's talking to whose self?

LA FLECHE. Who's picking on whom?

HARPAGON. I don't want you anywhere near me! You're always spying on me, every time I turn around, there you are, like a beanpole with huge bug eyes, looking here and there, looking for things to steal from me.

LA FLECHE. Look, let's be sensible about this. How could anyone steal so much as a carrot from you? You count the tomatoes on the vines out there every day! Everything else you have is locked up, hidden and guarded night and day!

HARPAGON. *(overheard aside)* Has he seen me in the garden?

LA FLECHE. Have I seen you where?

HARPAGON. Nowhere! Nowhere! I bet it's you who told everybody I have money hidden in the house.

LA FLECHE. You have money hidden in the house!?

HARPAGON. Who said that!?

LA FLECHE. Said what?

HARPAGON. That there's money hidden in the house!

LA FLECHE. There is!?

HARPAGON. I didn't say that!

LA FLECHE. Oh yes you did!

HARPAGON. *(getting confused)* You're deliberately confusing me.

LA FLECHE. Yes, and I do it so well, don't I?

HARPAGON. You keep your mouth shut out there. I don't want you spreading rumors that I have money hidden all over the place. Robbers will be crawling everywhere.

LA FLECHE. Please. It's common knowledge. There are people, on this very street, who are losing their homes, their livelihoods, everything, and they wonder why you're not suffering like they are. So they speculate.

HARPAGON. Well, they're wrong. I'm as poor as everybody else. I don't know how we'll make it through this year, this month. Put food in my children's mouths. Well, not for much longer. I'm going to marry them off! A rich husband for Elise, a rich wife for Cleante, and I'll save a fortune in food, clothing, horses– I can rent out their rooms!

LA FLECHE. And who will clean your house and take care of you? You're no…spring chicken. Oh, chicken, when was the last time we had a fowl for dinner, instead of a foul dinner? A plague on stinginess and people who live by it.

HARPAGON. What was that!?

LA FLECHE. What was what?

HARPAGON. What you just said?

LA FLECHE. What did I just say?

HARPAGON. Something about stinginess.

LA FLECHE. Did I?

HARPAGON. Didn't you? I heard you!

LA FLECHE. Well then, I guess I said it.

HARPAGON. Said what?

LA FLECHE. What?

HARPAGON. What you said!

LA FLECHE. What did I *say*?

HARPAGON. Yes!

LA FLECHE. I said yes?

HARPAGON. No!

LA FLECHE. No?

HARPAGON. You're doing it again!

LA FLECHE. What am I doing!

HARPAGON. Driving me mad, you—you cockroach!

LA FLECHE. Sou-scraper!

HARPAGON. Imbecile!

LA FLECHE. Warthog!

HARPAGON. Dolt!

LA FLECHE. Selfish, tight-fisted old fool! *(aside)* This is a useful exchange. *(to* **HARPAGON***)* Conversations that don't provide true communication or useful information are a waste of time and energy. I'm going outside to await your son's further instructions.

(The doorbell rings.)

HARPAGON. Ah, that's the marriage broker I called. Send her in on your way out.

LA FLECHE. I couldn't do that. I'm only an imbecile! *(aside)* But this imbecile is going to hang around, spy, and report to my master! *(He hides behind a screen.)*

HARPAGON. Never mind. Knowing Frosine, she'll come in anyway.

*(**HARPAGON** goes to his desk, takes out some papers, and talks to the audience)*

You know, it's very nerve-wracking keeping a huge sum of money in one's house. But where else is it safe these days? Clever is the man who can find the perfect hiding place for such an amount. Forget about safes! That's the first place they go. Stuffed in the mattress? They'll just as soon stab you in the middle of the night, then stab the mattress and take it all, leaving you to bleed to death. But the garden is worrisome too! One stray dog who likes the smell of gold and pfft! I'm barely sleeping at night. Every little moan and groan that the house makes and I'm on my feet with a shovel, ready to attack. Oh, how's a man to live any more with even a little peace of mind!? Whoops! Madame Frosine. I hope she didn't overhear!

*(**FROSINE** enters, shabby chic.)*

Madame Frosine! How long have you been there?

FROSINE. *(making a grand entrance)* Monsieur Harpagon! I just arrived. And what a pleasure to see you!

HARPAGON. And you. You—uh—didn't hear anything unusual as you came in?

FROSINE. You were mumbling something about gardens. I love gardens, don't you? And you have such a delightful one!

HARPAGON. Yes, it's all right. We get vegetables from it. Just vegetables. That's all. Nothing but vegetables. I mean, what else would there be in a garden?

FROSINE. Oh come now, you know what else!

HARPAGON. No, I don't!

FROSINE. Why, flowers, monsieur! Beautiful flowers to give to a lady who tickles your fancy.

HARPAGON. My fancy doesn't need any more tickling. I'm done with that.

FROSINE. I don't believe it. Why look at you, you're the picture of health. I swear, you look younger and more virile every day.

HARPAGON. I do?

FROSINE. I know a few thirty year olds who look and act older than you.

HARPAGON. But I'm past sixty! Well, just a little.

FROSINE. The prime of life! You must tell me your secret.

HARPAGON. I don't eat much.

FROSINE. Ah, I must try that some time.

HARPAGON. Yes, you should. You'd be surprised how much money you'll save.

FROSINE. Oh money! If you only knew the trouble I'm having—

HARPAGON. Yes, aren't we all? But let's discuss our business. I sent for you because—

FROSINE. You want to remarry!

HARPAGON. Who, me!?

FROSINE. I saw it in your eyes the minute I walked in. That gleam, that fire that says only one thing.

HARPAGON. Me!?

FROSINE. Why not? Give me your hand.

HARPAGON. YOU!?

FROSINE. No, silly goose. Three husbands were enough for me. Although, monsieur Harpagon, when I look at you, I'm sorely tempted! Now, let me see your life line. I'm an expert at these things. There, you see?

(She runs her nail across his hand and halfway up his arm. It tickles and he laughs.)

FROSINE. My, my my! It just goes on and on! You're going to live to be 120!

HARPAGON. I am?

FROSINE. Absolutely. And you'll want someone to care for you, and tend your house, and see to your every little need.

HARPAGON. I hadn't thought about that. I was thinking about marrying off my children.

FROSINE. All the more reason for *you* to get married! You'll be all alone here, wandering through these lonely, empty rooms— *(aside)* What happened to all his furniture? I heard he was filthy rich. *(back to him)* And I can help you with all three arrangements.

HARPAGON. Well. Let's talk about the children first.

FROSINE. Ah, the children. Life's most precious gift. How sad you must be to lose them.

HARPAGON. Huh? Oh yes, sad, sad, very sad.

FROSINE. So, let us begin with your son. A beautiful young man, strapping, handsome, refined, he should be no problem.

HARPAGON. I want a rich widow for my son. Older, I think. Someone well-endowed.

FROSINE. Ah, your son likes the mature, full-figured woman.

HARPAGON. Well-endowed monetarily. I want him married to a rich woman who will…offer me a sizeable sum in exchange for my son and his…youthful gifts.

FROSINE. Oh. Very sensible. Hmm. A rich widow. I think I know just the woman. She's a bit older than he is, but she has been left very well off.

HARPAGON. Does she want to remarry? Some of them don't, you know.

FROSINE. Who wouldn't want a handsome, young, virile man on her arm at any age!? I'll have to send a note to her and see if she's available. You may remember her. She used to live next door to you years ago. Madame Poquelin. *(poke-lán)*

HARPAGON. I remember that name. There was a scandal in the family.

FROSINE. Yes, alas. They moved away when the eldest son ran off to become… an actor.

HARPAGON. Madame Poquelin. Get in touch with her immediately. She sounds perfect.

FROSINE. Indeed I will. You'll remember her the instant you see her. She has a…memorable face. That nose, that wart with the hairs, the pock marks, oh and remember that lisp!?

HARPAGON. I remember the family had money.

FROSINE. Now she has it.

HARPAGON. How nice for me—her!

FROSINE. *(aside)* My mother should have chosen more carefully when I married the first time. The old goat spent all his money at the casinos and left me holding the dice. *(to **HARPAGON**)* I'll send a message to her today. Now, as for your daughter–

HARPAGON. This one will be easy. Señor Anselme, living in the next street, is looking to take a young wife. He's seen Elise and likes what he sees. And he'll take her without a dowry.

FROSINE. Without a dowry! Ah, you are a most thrifty and frugal man, so sensible when it comes to money. No wonder you're so wealthy.

HARPAGON. Who says I'm wealthy?

FROSINE. Oh, no one in particular. I'm just guessing that a smart–

LA FLECHE. *(aside from behind the screen;* **FROSINE** *hears him.)* Stingy—

FROSINE. – Industrious man like you must have something stashed away for these rainy days we're all having.

HARPAGON. I wish I did! But my children, they cost me a fortune, and there's this house to run, and the servants to be paid, and the horses…

FROSINE. Yes, I've seen your horses. Have you sent for the vet yet? Must be some dreadful disease.

LA FLECHE. *(peeking out from behind the screen)* Starvation.

HARPAGON. So, you'll arrange everything?

FROSINE. The full package. Of course, you'll want to throw a little dinner party, for Señor Anselme, and the wealthy widow—if she says yes, and for your fiancée!

HARPAGON. Mine?

FROSINE. Yours. Come, sir, have you ever seen me involved in any matchmaking endeavor that I did not successfully, completely and perfectly conclude? The man or woman does not exist for whom I cannot find the most delectable, the most suitable, the most delightful partner. And I know just the girl for you.

HARPAGON. Girl?

FROSINE. Young, sweet, innocent, kind, beautiful—

HARPAGON. But I'm an older—middle-aged man.

FROSINE. Have you never heard of the young girl who looks for…papá? This one, monsieur, has seen you in the neighborhood, and is delighted, dare I say, ravished by what she has seen. *(aside)* God forgive me for such a lie. Her poor, frail invalid mother is worried about her future and needs her married to someone who will provide. And she's so beautiful and sweet, that I'm wagering even this old crab will have to melt. *(to him)* Believe me, monsieur, this is a match made in heaven!

HARPAGON. I suppose I am in good form.

FROSINE. No, superb form! She talks of nothing else! She wants a portrait of you!

HARPAGON. Very flattering. But, you know, I do have a touch of phlegm from time to time.

FROSINE. Phlegm! She adores a good, solid, phlegmy cough!

HARPAGON. Really? *(he demonstrates)*

FROSINE. Oh yes. That's what led me to think of you remarrying. I spoke to her of the possibility and she went nearly mad with joy. *(aside)* Well, her mother did. That's not too much of a stretch.

HARPAGON. Mad with joy—think of it!

FROSINE. Yes, do think of it. Admired from afar, and soon to be near.

HARPAGON. I could send my horses and carriage for her.

FROSINE. *(aside)* Those horses couldn't pull a baby carriage! *(to him)* She would prefer to walk. She's a young, robust, healthy girl who loves exercise.

HARPAGON. Ah. Well, you've pointed out all her merits…

FROSINE. And they are many—

HARPAGON. Except you haven't mentioned—

FROSINE. Her name! Of course. It's Marianne.

LA FLECHE. *(again peeking out)* Uh-oh. Could there be two?

HARPAGON. Marianne. Very nice. I meant…the dowry.

FROSINE. The dowry!? *(aside)* The dowry! How shall I parlay that!? *(to him)* A minimum of twelve thousand a year!

LA FLECHE. *(out again)* Thank God. It's not her.

HARPAGON. Twelve thousand a year!? In gold, of course?

FROSINE. Better than gold. Much better than gold.

HARPAGON. What's better than gold?

FROSINE. First of all, she was raised in a household where expenditures on food were minimal. A little salad, a bit of milk, a few apples, consequently you'll save a good two thousand per year on food. Plus she cooks brilliantly with whatever she's given, so you can fire your cook and save another two thousand a year. In addition, she has no interest whatsoever in the latest fashion, can get by with two old gowns—one for weekdays and one for Sundays. Detests jewels, thinks they're crass and ugly—another six thousand a year.

FROSINE. *(cont.)* She may need a few extra pairs of shoes, because she walks everywhere, and you won't need your carriage, what's that–fifteen hundred a year, driver, footmen, and the like? Let's see, what else? Hates the gaming tables, never goes, never plays, that'll save you a good thousand a year—you know how women these days are flocking to the casinos. It's such a wonderful escape from our financial troubles. But she! She prefers to stay at home and....knit socks for her dear, darling husband. Do the math.

LA FLECHE. *(out again)* It's her. My master's true love.

HARPAGON. *(goes to his desk and scribbles, doing the math, while he talks)* One thousand, plus two, the jewels, the casino—carry the two...that's twelve thousand five hundred—you underestimated her!

FROSINE. So I did.

HARPAGON. You're right, Mme. Frosine. A poor girl is worth much more than a rich one. I'll take her!

FROSINE. I knew you would! Felicitations!

HARPAGON. Thank you.

FROSINE. I'll bring her over later with Señor Anselme and we'll have a jolly supper all together.

HARPAGON. A jolly supper? That's an awful lot of people to feed.

FROSINE. Well, she won't eat much! And you have such a beautiful garden from which to fill your table with all sorts of delicacies.

HARPAGON. THE GARDEN!? Oh, yes, the garden. Yes, I'll have my cook whip something up.

FROSINE. His last supper, eh?

HARPAGON. Oh yes, quite right. Won't need him any more! All right, bring the girl over, right away, so I can take a look at her.

FROSINE. Of course, monsieur. And I know the perfect marriage broker to draw up the papers. I'll send him over as well. We can get everything settled before the sun goes down.

HARPAGON. I like the way you work, Madame Frosine. No wasted time.

FROSINE. Exactly. Now, there's just one more thing...

HARPAGON. What's that?

FROSINE. A very small matter. *(She sits at his desk and scribbles a paper.)* My fee for brokering three marriages. I'm giving you a discount. Three for the price of two.

HARPAGON. Fee?

FROSINE. Yes, I said fee, not free.

HARPAGON. *(taking the paper and studying it as if it were infected)* Fee.

FROSINE. After all, monsieur, I'm a working woman, a widow who must fend for herself in the best way she can, and I can assure you, no one in town performs the service better than I. Besides, I find myself in temporary financial straits at the moment—who among us does not?—and so I'm asking only for the first half up front, the remainder to be paid when the marriage contracts are signed.

HARPAGON. Well, as it happens, I find myself a little short of funds as well—

FROSINE. Oh, when I think of how your fiancée longs to meet you face-to-face—

HARPAGON. Hard times have fallen upon all of us—

FROSINE. She can hardly wait for the wedding night—

HARPAGON. Rain! Do I hear rain!? *(He runs to the window.)*

FROSINE. Her sweet lips are already poised in a delicious pout, ready to kiss you—

HARPAGON. A heavy rain could wash things away—

FROSINE. All right. For you, I'll take a third up front–

HARPAGON. *(rushing out of the room)* Dinner! We'll settle everything at dinner!

FROSINE. *(to the audience)* Dinner my arse!

*(**LA FLECHE** appears from his hiding place.)*

LA FLECHE. I could have warned you—

FROSINE. You didn't have to. His reputation precedes him.

LA FLECHE. Don't hold your breath, waiting for your money.

FROSINE. Well, what shall I do!? I have to make a living somehow, and three brokered marriages would keep me going for months! Surely he has some money around here.

LA FLECHE. Oh, trust me, he does. And I'm going to find it. I've already narrowed down the playing field.

FROSINE. And when you do find it...

LA FLECHE. I'll make sure everybody gets their fair share, don't you worry. Your mother brokered my parents' marriage, and it was a very happy one.

FROSINE. A happy marriage! Well at least a few of them work out!

LA FLECHE. What makes you think that old goat's marriage will be happy?

FROSINE. How much longer could he live? She'll end up a rich young widow. Then she'll be happy.

LA FLECHE. Are you absolutely positive she wants to marry him?

FROSINE. Of course she doesn't! She's met some handsome young thing with no money, she doesn't even know his name but ping! They're in love, capital L, but she has to marry this—this—poor excuse for a human being because she has to look out for her—

BOTH. –Poor, frail, invalid mother.

FROSINE. Life can be so cruel.

*(Enter **MAITRE JACQUES**, very dejected, with a piece of paper.)*

LA FLECHE. Jacques! What are you doing out of the kitchen? Why aren't you making ze famous vegetable zoup?

MAITRE JACQUES. S'il vous plait, La Fleche, do not joke. I am too sad. I 'ate zees job.

FROSINE. Poor fellow. What's the problem?

MAITRE JACQUES. Ze boss, 'e send me out to deliver a message. 'e forget I am ze maitre. A chef extraordinaire. 'e force me to me make ze vegetable zoup every day. I am seek of eet! Zen 'e insult me by making me ze errand boy! And on ze way to and from zees errand, I pass le boucher, wiz ze beautiful, pink, plump sausages and pigs and chickens 'anging in ze window, zen le patisserie, wiz ze tartes, ze gateux, zen la boulangerie, wees all ze herbes and spices, ze fruits, and leetle delicacies all spread out for everyone—except me. Eet is sad. Zees 'ouse ees sad. I am sad.

FROSINE. Suddenly I'm very hungry! Excuse me! *(She exits.)*

LA FLECHE. Now look, my man, you just have to learn to stand up to him, like I do.

MAITRE JACQUES. Easy for you to say. 'e does not pay you.

LA FLECHE. Are you or are you not the greatest chef in all of France?

MAITRE JACQUES. I am, but no one knows it but me.

LA FLECHE. Well, you have to make them know it. Make him know it. Stand tall, proud, confident.

MAITRE JACQUES. Tall, proud confident...

(HARPAGON enters.)

HARPAGON. Ah, Jacques, good. You're back

MAITRE JACQUES. *(deflating)* 'ere is ze message from ze gentilhomme you sent me to. *(He starts to slink off.)*

HARPAGON. Just a minute! Come back here, Jacques.

(He does. **LA FLECHE** *pushes him forward.)*

MAITRE JACQUES. *Maitre* Jacques, s'il vous plait. I am ze chef.

HARPAGON. Yes, yes, my cook.

MAITRE JACQUES. *(with a nod to* **LA FLECHE***)* Votre *chef*, monsieur.

HARPAGON. All right, ze chef. You're going to prepare a dinner tonight.

LA FLECHE. *(aside to* **MAITRE JACQUES***)* Told you it would work!

MAITRE JACQUES. *(complete change of mood)* A dinner!? Enfin! At last! I am going to prepare un grand dinner! Oh, my 'eart, she weel burst with joie! Zere are cobwebs in ze keetchen from lack of créativité, my 'ands tweetch from not slicing, dicing, ricing, whipping, chipping, flipping, gripping ze sauté pans, from not peeling, congealing, kneeling, feeling ze dough plumping up in ze bowls, my nose droops weeth sadness from not smelling ze jelling of ze aspeec, my eyes weep, searching for the gloss of ze sauce, my mouth, my mouth is numb from not tasting ze markerel, ze pickerel, ze caramel, ze béchamel, ze chanterelle weeth just a soupçon of muscatel, oh merci, monsieur, I weel prepare for you un dinner sublime!

HARPAGON. *(aside)* I have to get rid of him.

MAITRE JACQUES. 'Ow many peoples?

HARPAGON. Let me see…eight, I think. Maybe ten

MAITRE JACQUES. Dix! Dix peoples! A banquet!

HARPAGON. Hold on now. We don't need a banquet, the king isn't coming. We can't afford meals like that—and make sure you cook for eight. Food for eight will feed ten. These are hard times.

MAITRE JACQUES. 'Ard times, oui, I 'ave 'heard about zees 'ard times many times in zees 'ouse. What you want me to prepare zees time? Ze same old vegetable zoup?

HARPAGON. Yes, but I suppose they'll want something more filling as well. Potatoes.

MAITRE JACQUES. Ah, ze pommes de terre, jardinière, weez camembert? Or chauffés, gratinés, sautés, flambés, soufflés, machés, purées, weez a delicate bouquet of cabernet? Oh, monsieur, I know my métier! I go deeg up ze potatoes right away!

HARPAGON. No! I'll deeg up–get the potatoes and bring them to you. Just keep it simple, no fancy sauces, meats, butter—

MAITRE JACQUES. Oh monsieur, you must 'ave butter!

HARPAGON. Oh, all right, a little butter.

MAITRE JACQUES. A leetle butter, oui! You weel see, Maitre Jacques weel make ze best, most delicious dinner of your life! *(to* **LA FLECHE***)* You were right!

(He exits, singing jubilantly.)

"Cooking is beauty, beauty is cooking, zat's all you know on earth, and all you need to know…"

HARPAGON. He's a madman. To get such pleasure from work! I don't understand the human race.

LA FLECHE. Perhaps because you're not a member of it.

(**HARPAGON** *tries to hit* **LA FLECHE** *with his cane, but* **LA FLECHE** *dodges him and exits.* **HARPAGON** *takes out the paper* **MAITRE JACQUES** *gave to him.*)

HARPAGON. Can't let that good-for-nothing distract me from my business. And look at this! This foreign money-lender already has a borrower for me! Of course, he is foreign. Can't trust foreigners. But he did come highly recommended. Have to risk it. Well, now, to the children. *(He goes to the wings and calls.)* Elise! Cleante! Get down here at once! You too, Valere!

(**ELISE** *and* **VALERE** *enter, disheveled, hair tousled.* **VALERE** *is wiping his mouth.*)

What the devil have you two been up to?

ELISE. Cleaning, father.

VALERE. Tidying up.

ELISE & VALERE. The house.

HARPAGON. Well, tidy up yourselves, I have news. And where is your brother?

ELISE. He should be back shortly. He went on…an errand.

HARPAGON. Never here when I want him, always around when I don't.

ELISE. We both try to do whatever you desire, father.

VALERE. Both of your children seem to be devoted to you, monsieur, at least that is what I have been able to observe in my short time here.

HARPAGON. Well, I'm glad to hear that, because there's something I desire them to do.

ELISE. Of course.

HARPAGON. Good. I want you to get married!

(**ELISE** *and* **VALERE** *look at each other, hardly daring to hope.*)

ELISE. Married!

HARPAGON. Yes, married. You're of age, why shouldn't you? Well, Valère, shouldn't she marry?

VALERE. I see...no reason why not, depending upon the choice of the...uh...spouse.

HARPAGON. Exactly. And I've found one.

VALERE & ELISE. Oh?

HARPAGON. Practically under our noses!

ELISE & VALERE. *(ever more hopeful)* Really!?

HARPAGON. You'll have to admit, finally, that you have a very clever father. Smart and sensible in all things.

ELISE. I've always thought so, father.

VALERE. Yes, she's told me that many times.

HARPAGON. He's the perfect husband for you. Well, a bit older...

ELISE. A bit?

VALERE. How much of a bit?

HARPAGON. A mere thirty-five years.

ELISE. Wh—who—who—!!

HARPAGON. What's the matter with you? You sound like a pigeon!

ELISE. I thought—at least I was hoping—

VALERE *(interrupting)* And what is the name of this fifty-five-year-old gentleman, if we may ask?

HARPAGON. Señor Anselme.

ELISE. Who?

HARPAGON. Señor Anselme. He lives in the next block. He's seen you and he likes what he sees!

ELISE. But- but- but-I haven't seen him!

HARPAGON. You will.

ELISE. No, I don't think so.

HARPAGON. Why not?

ELISE. Because I'm going to be sick!

(She sinks into a chair. **VALERE** *tries to comfort her without* **HARPAGON** *seeing.)*

HARPAGON. Nonsense. You're as fit as I am.

ELISE. Father, I don't wish to marry.

HARPAGON. Daughter, I don't care. It's all being arranged and you're getting married. Tonight, if I can get a judge over here after the dinner. Frosine is sending a marriage broker over to draw up the contracts.

ELISE. No!

HARPAGON. No?

ELISE. No! I will not marry Señor ants-whatever-his-name-is.

HARPAGON. Oh yes you will! I'm your father and you do as I say!

ELISE. I'm your daughter and I won't! You can't make me!

HARPAGON. I beg to differ, but I can.

ELISE. I'd rather go into a convent!

HARPAGON. No convents! There's a huge entry fee!

ELISE. Then I'll take poison and die!

HARPAGON. You won't die. I won't hear of it. And you will marry him. Who ever heard of a daughter talking to her father like this!

ELISE. Who ever heard of a father forcing his daughter to marry like this!

HARPAGON. All fathers do it. Besides, it's a completely suitable match.

ELISE. It is not!

HARPAGON. Is!

ELISE. Not! *(She screams.)*

HARPAGON. Stop that, or I'll take the stick to you!

(He chases her around the room until he's worn out.)

When I catch you...

(He finally collapses in the ratty, uncomfortable chair. **VALERE** *takes* **ELISE** *aside.)*

VALERE. You have to learn to play him! Stay calm.

ELISE. *(to* **VALERE***)* Calm down!? Is that all you can say!? *(to* **HARPAGON***)* Father, why don't you ask Valere? You value his opinion so much, why not ask him what he thinks about this marriage?

HARPAGON. And you'll abide by his decision?

ELISE. Yes. I will.

HARPAGON. All right. Valere, what do you think?

VALERE. You're giving a dinner?

HARPAGON. Yes. Why do you look so surprised?

VALERE. Oh, just that you've never given one, not since I've been here, at any rate. Not that the vegetable soup isn't delicious and filling…

HARPAGON. Well, I'm giving one tonight. And we're having potatoes too!

VALERE. How very generous. Who is coming?

ELISE. Valere! My father asked your opinion about the marriage. *(She keeps trying to interject a comment through the next exchange.)*

VALERE. Yes, of course. Well. I think—

HARPAGON. There's a great deal of preparation to be handled. I'm leaving all that to you, my trusted valet, Valere. I want you to serve the meal.

VALERE. I'll see to everything. But, you know, monsieur, I have only one uniform and it has a huge stain on the front…

HARPAGON. Stand like this, with your hat like this, to hide it.

VALERE. Yes, a brilliant idea. Now, there's just the problem of my breeches. There are holes on both sides. What do we do about that?

ELISE. *(completely out of patience)* VALERE!

HARPAGON. *(to* **ELISE***)* Stop interrupting. *(to* **VALERE***)* Stand with your back to the buffet, I'll have that good-for-nothing La Fleche serve the platters which you will hand to him. Good God, do I have to do the thinking for everybody around here!?

VALERE. Well, monsieur, it's just that no one has a keener mind, a quicker wit, a sharper tongue—

HARPAGON. What!?

VALERE. A sharper tongue for cutting through the bull… dogging problems of life and finding perfect solutions.

HARPAGON. Yes, that's true. So I take it you approve of my marriage plan for Elise?

VALERE. She is... a girl to be married without further delay.

HARPAGON. Hah! You hear that!? Tonight!

VALERE. Although, if I may suggest, monsieur, a girl gets married only once in her life, and perhaps she might need a little time to prepare, find a wedding dress, fix her hair—

ELISE. Exactly! I need time!

HARPAGON. Why should she do all that!? Needless expense.

VALERE. True. But then there's the marriage night. Her mother is not here to explain to her the...intricacies of the marriage bed.

HARPAGON. Bah. Nothing to it. Anselme will show her everything.

*(***ELISE*** faints. ***VALERE*** revives her.)*

VALERE. She's overwhelmed with joy at the thought.

HARPAGON. She should be. When he dies, she'll inherit everything. He lost his family several years ago, and he has no living relatives.

VALERE. Wonderful. But perhaps he might not want to rush into things.

HARPAGON. He's as eager as a young buck in heat. And he'll take her without a dowry.

VALERE. Oh well, without a dowry, that's something. However, I've heard it said that one should give a little consideration to the feelings of the young lady in question—

HARPAGON. Without a dowry...

VALERE. Ah, truly an incontestable argument. Of course the age difference could make for problems—

HARPAGON. No dowry!

VALERE. *(starting to lose it)* It's the determining factor. No doubt about it. Yet, I can't help thinking how many fathers there are out there who are more concerned with their daughters' happiness than with the amount of money they're going to get when they BARTER HER IN TRADE! Fathers who wouldn't ever think of sacrificing their daughters at the altar of greed, fathers who strive for marriages well-suited to both parties, where peace and harmony co-exist—

HARPAGON. HE DOESN'T WANT A DOWRY!

VALERE. *(barely holding it together)* Well, what can one say? Without a dowry says it all.

HARPAGON. *(to* **ELISE***)* There, you see? Valere agrees with me. There's no more to be said.

(A dog barks.)

What's that! There's a dog in the garden! That damned neighbor's nuisance of a cur! GET OUT OF THERE! STAY AWAY FROM MY GOLD—POTATOES! *(to them)* Gold potatoes. It's a new strain from Ireland. Very hardy.

(He exits into the garden. **VALERE** *throws a fit, punches a pillow on the shabby sofa.)*

VALERE. Was there ever such a man!?

ELISE. That's the way you defend me!? You practically threw me on to the altar!

VALERE. What could I do!? I had to placate him! Resistance toward someone like that merely aggravates his natural, ingrained, miserable, narrow-minded INFLEXIBILITY! *(calming himself down)* So, no matter what I say, you must remember that I want only your happiness and mine.

ELISE. But this marriage!

VALERE. We'll find a way to stop it.

ELISE. We don't have a whole lot of time…

VALERE. You'll get sick.

ELISE. I AM sick!

VALERE. No, you'll pretend a grave illness. We'll paint your face gray or something.

ELISE. He'll call a doctor.

VALERE. Are you kidding? That would cost him money!

ELISE. Good point.

HARPAGON. *(re-entering, with the potatoes)* Damn dog. *(He counts the potatoes.)* Let me see—six potatoes for ten people. That's more than half a potato per person!

VALERE. *(to* **ELISE***)* As I was saying, young lady, a daughter has to cater to her father's wishes, no matter what they are. The husband's age is of no importance, his looks are a mere trifle. When a girl finds a husband willing to take her without a dowry, she must accept and obey.

HARPAGON. Very nicely put, my lad.

VALERE. Oh, pardon me, monsieur, I should not have spoken to her out of turn.

HARPAGON. Nonsense. I give you leave to speak to her, instruct her, keep her in tow, in fact, you are now in charge of my daughter. And you, young lady, will obey his every command.

VALERE. Did you her that, Elise? My word is law.

ELISE. Yes, sir.

VALERE. Monsieur, I shall follow her constantly, and continue to advise her on this very subject of marriage until she sees the wisdom of it.

HARPAGON. Good man, good man. Have to go give these to the cook. *(He exits.)*

VALERE. And I have to prepare for our banquet. And you must follow me everywhere!

(They exit, **VALERE** *chasing* **ELISE***. Enter* **CLEANTE** *and* **LA FLECHE.** *)*

CLEANTE. *(looking around)* Good, father's not around. Now, tell me everything.

LA FLECHE. I found a money-lender for you.

CLEANTE. I knew you would! Oh joy, oh rapture! Because, you know, the situation has grown much more urgent. I have seen Marianne— *(bursting into song again)* Marianne, Marianne, oh my dear Marianne—

LA FLECHE. *(slapping him)* Stay on target.

CLEANTE. Oh, right. Well, her mother has arranged a marriage for her!

LA FLECHE. No! What a surprise!

CLEANTE. Yes! Through Frosine, that dreadful marriage broker!

LA FLECHE. *(aside)* I can't tell him myself. It's too…heartbreaking.

CLEANTE. And I have to get her over here so I can prove that I'm the better choice, and then she can go and tell her poor, frail, invalid mother that she's met someone better. I've ordered some furniture and things to be delivered and I have to pay for them when they get here!

LA FLECHE. Not to worry. The broker I found is going to arrange a loan for you.

CLEANTE. La Fleche, you are a treasure! Remind me to give you a raise, if I ever have enough money to do it.

LA FLECHE. Thank you, master.

CLEANTE. Now, who is this broker?

LA FLECHE. *(pulling a legal document from a pocket)* He has an excellent reputation. He made contact with a wealthy man willing to lend you enough money to make a lasting impression on Marianne, her poor, frail, invalid mother and the whole neighborhood.

CLEANTE. Oh! I knew a positive attitude would hold me in good stead. Can you get the full fifteen thousand!?

LA FLECHE. Yes, and at only five percent interest.

CLEANTE. Five percent!? Who's the lender?

LA FLECHE. He wouldn't say yet. We'll find out soon enough. But, there's one little glitch.

CLEANTE. A glitch? What kind of glitch?

LA FLECHE. It's a clause in the contract. In very small print.

CLEANTE. A clause? What does it say?

LA FLECHE. It says— *(He whips out a huge magnifier and reads slowly.)* Now, therefore, whereas the party of the second part *non corpus mentalia*, which shall without the necessity of *coram robis*, be constituted for the party of the first part, hereinafter to indemnify at thirty-five percent, be a *tort feaser* and without the requisite notice be declared to be in default, resisting the replevin of chattels a fortiori, and immediate *habeas corpus*.

CLEANTE. Uh-huh. What does that mean?

LA FLECHE. I have no idea. But I didn't like the sound of that thirty-five percent.

CLEANTE. Oh, I'm in despair! I can't trust a loan document I can't read. Do you know any lawyers?

LA FLECHE. Alas, no. I've tried to avoid them most of my life.

CLEANTE. La Fleche, you *have* to find the cashbox. We need the backup. The money lender might turn me down! You have to hide and watch my father and figure out where it is and get it without him seeing you, and before tonight!

LA FLECHE. No problem! *(aside)* WHAT!!?? I know approximately where it is, but how to get it without him seeing me…?

(the voice of **HARPAGON** *from offstage)*

CLEANTE. Here he comes! Go hide! Now!

(Once again **LA FLECHE** *goes behind the screen.* **HARPAGON** *enters.)*

HARPAGON. There you are, you worthless ninny! Where have you been?

CLEANTE. Nowhere in particular. Out for some exercise. You're always telling me to walk, so I went for a walk.

HARPAGON. Good. Looks like you're in a mood to be obedient.

CLEANTE. Obedient?

HARPAGON. That's right. I want to talk to you about…marriage.

CLEANTE. Marriage! What a wonderful topic!

HARPAGON. Good. For once we think alike.

CLEANTE. Oh yes, father, we do.

HARPAGON. Now, it so happens there's a young lady who recently moved into the neighborhood. On this street, in fact. Her name is…uh…something with an M…

CLEANTE. Marianne?

HARPAGON. Oh, you know her.

CLEANTE. Oh yes, I've met her, in fact!

HARPAGON. *(aside)* Good. Now I can find out if Frosine was exaggerating or not. *(to him)* Well, what's your opinion? What do you think of her?

CLEANTE. She's magnificent! Delightful.

HARPAGON. What's she look like?

CLEANTE. Beautiful. No, beyond beautiful. She has the sparkle of a waterfall with the afternoon sun thrown upon it, the whimsy of a butterfly flitting across a meadow of asphodels, the serenity of a mountain lake at dusk—

HARPAGON. Oh shut up! What about her behavior? Her demeanor?

CLEANTE. Perfect. No question about it. Modest, respectful, yet with a *je ne sais quoi*—a fire in her, or a light, something intangible yet very palpable, that suggests spring bursting forth anew.

HARPAGON. *(aside)* How did I spawn this creature? *(to him)* So you think a girl like that should be taken seriously.

CLEANTE. Very seriously.

HARPAGON. And she would be an advantageous match?

CLEANTE. The most advantageous match any man could make!

HARPAGON. What about as a good house-keeper? Cooking, sewing, cleaning…

CLEANTE. She is unsurpassed.

HARPAGON. And whomever she married could consider himself a lucky man?

CLEANTE. *(over the moon)* The luckiest man alive!

HARPAGON. She's not rich, you know.

CLEANTE. What does money matter when a woman of her accomplishments is being considered!?

HARPAGON. I'm not convinced. But, Frosine did point out how a poor woman will expect less—

CLEANTE. Exactly!

HARPAGON. Well, all right. Then we are agreed.

CLEANTE. Completely in agreement! Oh father, I am the happiest man alive!

HARPAGON. Yes, well, I suppose I will be too, when I marry her.

CLEANTE. Absolutely! When you— *(He freezes for a long moment, letting it sink in, then laughs.)* Father, this is funny. You said "I" instead of "you."

HARPAGON. Said what?

CLEANTE. Said "When I marry her, instead of "When you marry her."

HARPAGON. That's right. When I marry her.

CLEANTE. Meaning me, of course.

HARPAGON. No, meaning me, of course.

CLEANTE. But you're not marrying her—I am.

HARPAGON. No, you're not. I am marrying...what's-her-name.

CLEANTE. Marrying Marianne? You're joking.

HARPAGON. When have you ever known me to joke?

CLEANTE. Once, when I was very little.

HARPAGON. I'm glad you're so impressed with her. She'll be your new mother.

CLEANTE. *(aside)* I'm nauseous. My knees are turning to water. It's a dream. It must be a dream. *(He slaps his own face.)* Ow! It's not a dream. He must be the one Frosine made the match with! It can't be!

HARPAGON. But don't you worry about being left out in the cold. I have arranged a marriage for you as well.

CLEANTE. Me? Oh God, no.

HARPAGON. Do you remember that lovely lady who was such a good friend of your mother?

CLEANTE. Mother had a lot of friends.

HARPAGON. Madame Poquelin.

CLEANTE. Poke-who?

HARPAGON. Poquelin. She used to live next door to us.

CLEANTE. Poke—poke—Poquelin! The one with the—the—face, with the wart with the hairs growing out of it? The one with the lisp!?

HARPAGON. Good. You remember. She's extremely wealthy.

CLEANTE. She's extremely ugly! And old!

HARPAGON. What does that matter?

CLEANTE. It doesn't MATTER!? Good, then you can marry the warthog and I'll take Marianne!

HARPAGON. Don't be ridiculous. I'm marrying Marianne and you are marrying Mme. Poquelin. I'm now completely convinced that my marrying a poor innocent girl who will expect very little is what I should do, and marrying a rich one is best for you, and all your expensive tastes. Frosine is bringing the girl over shortly to meet me.

CLEANTE. Over my dead body.

HARPAGON. What did you say!

CLEANTE. You heard me. Over my dead body will I allow either of these marriages to take place. I'll move heaven and earth, I'll walk through fire, I'll—

HARPAGON. You'll shut up and do as you're told. What is this, Revolt of the Children week!?

CLEANTE. *(He starts to exit, then stops and turns.)* You are… despicable! There, I've said it. To my own father.

HARPAGON. I am not despicable. I'm sensible. It's for your own good. You'll have a secure future and I won't have to worry about how I'm going to provide for you—or Elise. It's the right thing to do.

(**HARPAGON** *exits.*)

CLEANTE. *(dragging* **LA FLECHE** *from behind the screen by the ear)* Did you know this!?

(**LA FLECHE** *nods his bowed head.*)

CLEANTE. You knew! You knew and you didn't tell me!?

LA FLECHE. I couldn't bear to be the one who broke the wretched news!

CLEANTE. Well, what does it matter, my life is over. My positive attitude is gone, I'm desolate, stricken, numb, what else?

LA FLECHE. Wounded—

CLEANTE. Wounded—

LA FLECHE. Bereft—

CLEANTE. Bereft—

LA FLECHE. In total despair—

CLEANTE. That's enough! I can't take on any more!

LA FLECHE. Now, my good and kind master, I want you to take a deep breath.

(He tries and sighs.)

LA FLECHE. *(cont.)* Try again. Come on. A nice, deep breath.

(a little more success)

And pull yourself together. I have a plan. And I need you to be completely focused so you can help me achieve success.

CLEANTE. All right. What is it?

LA FLECHE. I think I know where his money is.

CLEANTE. *(complete mood swing)* YOU KNOW WHERE IT IS!!!???

*(**LA FLECHE** claps his hand over **CLEANTE**'s mouth.)*

(mumbling) Where is it?

LA FLECHE. Never mind. It's better if you don't know. You'll say or do something, give a little glance, a small slip of the tongue, and you'll give me away. Your job will be to keep your father distracted so I can steal it.

CLEANTE. Stealing from my own father. I never believed it would come to this.

LA FLECHE. It's just for a little while. You're going to give it back. Well, most of it.

CLEANTE. I am? Oh, of course I am.

LA FLECHE. After a few expenses are subtracted from the total. Just leave everything to me, and whatever you do, keep him in this room and diverted by something. Can you do that?

CLEANTE. Yes! Anything to win the hand of my— *(singing again)* Marianne, Marianne, oh my dear—

LA FLECHE *(slapping again)* Stop. Focus. Work with me.

CLEANTE. Keep him in this room and divert him with something.

LA FLECHE. And that something will be—

CLEANTE. Yes?

LA FLECHE. *(aside)* He can be really dim at times. *(He gives him a good hard stare, finally hums the Marianne song.)*

LA FLECHE & CLEANTE. Marianne!

LA FLECHE. Frosine is bringing her over. Any minute now.

CLEANTE. But the furniture hasn't arrived!

LA FLECHE. If she is the sweet, simple, modest, wholesome, kindhearted, gentle, caring creature we've all heard about, she won't even see the bare walls. She'll see only you. Now, go get ready to greet her.

CLEANTE. Yes, you're right! Who cares for furniture! I must go and spruce up! *(He exits, on the wings of love.)*

LA FLECHE. All right, now to the task at hand.

(He exits, we hear rattling of metal backstage, and he re-enters with a shovel.)

Once more, unto the screen, dear friends, once more. And wait for the right moment..

*(He goes back behind the screen, as **HARPAGON** enters with **MAITRE SIMON**, both in an agitated state.)*

HARPAGON. Maitre Simon, I am simply asking you to give me a few pointers, just a little push in the direction of my becoming a money-lender like yourself.

LA FLECHE. *(aside, head out from behind the screen)* Maitre Simon!? Uh-oh. *(back behind the screen)*

MAITRE SIMON. Yes, you are asking me to train you to go into competition with me! To give you lessons that took me years of hard work and mistakes and misery and failures and starving and suffering to get me where I am today. I'll be creating another competitor! This deserves no less than the highest compensation.

HARPAGON. I am absolutely willing to pay for such information.

MAITRE SIMON. How much?

HARPAGON. Well, that depends. Are we talking about a one-time service fee, an hourly rate, a money-back guarantee if I am not successful, a fee when it is evident that I am successful...

MAITRE SIMON. I accept only a one-time, up-front, no money-back guarantee fee of...

(He looks around the shabby room, pretends to calculate with an abacus, and speaks aside.)

I heard this man was rich! I need some extra income, things are very, very bad out there! Ten percent unemployment, banks closing left and right, nobody trusts anybody! They say he has a fortune hidden away—have you heard anything about that? How much should I bleed him for?

(back to **HARPAGON***)*

MAITRE SIMON. *(cont.)* Well, monsieur, I think I could give you a very good deal for, let us say...five hundred in gold.

HARPAGON. *(aside)* Oh, this is not going to be easy. *(to* **MAITRE SIMON***)* Oh, my poor heart! I cannot afford such a staggering amount as that! I need to learn your trade to earn some money because, as you see, we have so little here at the moment! Practically starving we are. Two children to feed and clothe, and have you seen my horses?

MAITRE SIMON. Yes, indeed I have. Horsemeat can be very tasty when prepared correctly.

HARPAGON. I...might be able to scrape together one hundred...

MAITRE SIMON. For you, I could be persuaded to come down to four–

HARPAGON. Perhaps two–

MAITRE SIMON. Three–

HARPAGON. Done.

MAITRE SIMON. Deal.

HARPAGON. So, where do we start?

MAITRE SIMON. With a client, of course.

HARPAGON. A client! How do I find one?

MAITRE SIMON. It so happens I have one which I will pass on to you for an extra sixty–

HARPAGON. Twenty–

MAITRE SIMON. Forty–

HARPAGON. Thirty–

MAITRE SIMON. Done.

HARPAGON. Deal. Who is he?

MAITRE SIMON. I don't know.

HARPAGON. You have a client and you don't know who it is?

MAITRE SIMON. Yes, a client! And we both will meet him very soon!

HARPAGON. How do you know you have one if you don't know who he is!? This is a very strange business, money-lending.

MAITRE SIMON. Monsieur Harpagon, have you never heard of an intermediary? This is the first lesson of money-lending. You talk to the person the borrower sends. You size the fellow up and decide, with impeccable judgment, which I always have, if the person he represents will pay the money back. Then you meet the person and you have two people to judge from.

HARPAGON. And from two meetings you're absolutely sure that there's no risk involved? Do you know the family name? Financial standing? Background? How much does he want?

MAITRE SIMON. Fifteen thousand, and no, I don't have all the details yet. It so happens this client's intermediary appeared just today. Better to discover all that from the horse's mouth. What I can tell you is that his family is very rich, the mother is deceased, leaving him a small income, but the father has enormous wealth, and probably won't live through this year.

HARPAGON. Well, that is very good to hear. So set up a meeting immediately. I'm very anxious to get this new business going–

CLEANTE. *(entering)* Father, guess who is about to arrive–! *(seeing* **MAITRE SIMON** *)* Oh, excuse me.

HARPAGON. Go away, I'm conducting business.

MAITRE SIMON. Now, now, if this is your son, I want to meet him. He looks like an upstanding sort.

HARPAGON. He's a rattle-brained saphead.

MAITRE SIMON. At your service, monsieur.

CLEANTE. Thank you, monsieur. What service might that be?

MAITRE SIMON. I bring people together for the purpose of exchanging money. I'm conducting just that for your father.

CLEANTE. *(aside)* Useful information for me right now!

HARPAGON. Don't bother him with talk of money. He knows nothing about it.

CLEANTE. Perhaps because no one ever took the time to instruct me.

HARPAGON. I certainly did! I tried, Maitre Simon, believe me I tried!

CLEANTE. Yes, once, when I was very little.

HARPAGON. And you were completely hopeless!

CLEANTE. I was five years old!

HARPAGON. No excuse.

MAITRE SIMON. Perhaps if he listens to us, he will learn something. No extra charge! *(aside)* For now.

CLEANTE. I'd like to learn about this business, as it happens.

HARPAGON. Oh all right! Now, Maitre Simon, I'm sure the young man who wishes to borrow fifteen thousand from me is much more level-headed than my son, so I'm inclined to make a deal with him.

CLEANTE. Fifteen thousand? *(The light bulb goes off.)*

HARPAGON. At how much interest?

MAITRE SIMON. Well, there's a clause in very small print that only a lawyer can read.

HARPAGON. And?

MAITRE SIMON. One hundred dollar late fee, and the interest goes up to thirty-five percent if there's a missed payment, and the first payment is due within one week, a surcharge for administering and keeping the books on the loan–

CLEANTE. *(aside)* A clause in very small print? Thirty-five percent? It's me! It's him! It's a mess!

LA FLECHE. *(from behind the screen, as* **HARPAGON** *reads the clause)* Pssst!

*(***CLEANTE*** slowly backs up to the screen.)*

Don't let him know you know! Not yet!

*(***CLEANTE*** moves forward again, listening intently.)*

HARPAGON. Very clever. Very clever indeed. Mightn't the young man figure it out? We couldn't be so lucky as to find someone as dimwitted as my son.

CLEANTE. *(to his father, barely hiding his anger)* Well, father, if it were me, and I couldn't pay it back, Maitre Simon would come after you and have you arrested!

MAITRE SIMON. *(enjoying the joke)* I would indeed! What a joke that would be!

*(***MAITRE SIMON*** and* **CLEANTE** *laugh.* **HARPAGON** *does not see the humor.)*

CLEANTE. *(laughing and angry, unable to stand the pretense any longer)* Fifteen thousand? At thirty-five percent to be paid back in one week!? Your client would have to be as lame-brained as you think I am to accept such terms!

MAITRE SIMON. True!

CLEANTE. True!

HARPAGON. *(getting it)* You!?

MAITRE SIMON. Him?

CLEANTE. Me!

MAITRE SIMON. Ai!

HARPAGON. Wait a minute, wait a minute. You are the young man who wants to bleed me dry?

CLEANTE. And you are the skinflint who lets his children starve and forces them to look elsewhere for financial aid!?

MAITRE SIMON. And this is a family squabble I don't want to be in the middle of!? *(to **HARPAGON**)* Believe me, Monsieur Harpagon, I did not know who the young man was, or that he was attached to you in any way whatsoever.

HARPAGON. Some moneylender you are!

CLEANTE. Some father you are!

LA FLECHE. *(stepping out briefly from the screen and grabbing **CLEANTE**)* Go along with him! Placate him! Distract him! Bring in the girl!

*(**LA FLECHE** goes back behind the screen. **CLEANTE** takes a deep breath.)*

CLEANTE. Well! Ha, ha ha. This is a joke on both of us.

HARPAGON. I don't see the humor in a son who wants to ruin himself with disgraceful borrowing.

MAITRE SIMON. *(aside)* At outrageously elevated interest!

CLEANTE. You're right, father. I was being greedy. I don't know where I picked up that trait. But let's forget all about it. I don't need the money after all.

MAITRE SIMON. So I guess the deal is off?

CLEANTE. Yes, I've decided to go in another direction.

MAITRE SIMON. And you don't want to lend?

HARPAGON. To my own son!? I should say not.

MAITRE SIMON. Well, then, if I may just present my fee…

HARPAGON. For brokering a deal between a father and his own son? That didn't go through?

MAITRE SIMON. A fee is a fee, no matter who is involved, or whether the deal goes through. Time is money.

HARPAGON. Not this time it isn't! You won't get a sou out of me!

(**LA FLECHE** *peeks out from behind the screen, as* **MAITRE SIMON** *and* **HARPAGON** *get into a shouting match.*)

LA FLECHE. The perfect moment!

(He sneaks into the garden. Periodically, we see dirt being thrown in the air.)

MAITRE SIMON. Now, just a minute!

HARPAGON. Not another second! You'll probably charge me for it!

MAITRE SIMON. I'll take you to court!

HARPAGON. I'll take you back!

MAITRE SIMON. You're every bit the skinflint people told me you were!

HARPAGON. And you're a—a—a— ninnyhammer! *(aside)* I'm running out of insults.

FROSINE. *(entering with a very reluctant* **MARIANNE***)* Bonjour, Monsieur Harpagon! I've brought you your prize!

MARIANNE. *(seeing* **CLEANTE***)* OH!

CLEANTE. AH!

MARIANNE. *(aside to* **FROSINE***)* Frosine!

FROSINE. What?

MARIANNE. *(pointing to* **CLEANTE***)* It's he!

FROSINE. Who?

MARIANNE. He!

FROSINE. Him?

MARIANNE. Yes!

FROSINE. No.

MARIANNE. Yes!

FROSINE. Oh.

MARIANNE. What is he doing here?

FROSINE. He lives here! You didn't know?

MARIANNE. Know what?

FROSINE. He's the son of the man you're engaged to marry.

MARIANNE. Ewww.

FROSINE. I quite agree. You had no idea where he was from?

MARIANNE. Only that he lived in the neighborhood.

FROSINE. Like father, like son. How will this fadge?

(CLEANTE rushes to MARIANNE, takes her arm and presents her to his father)

CLEANTE. Father! Look who's here!

HARPAGON. Who's that?

CLEANTE. It's your –ugh–fiancée!

MARIANNE. But you—I—he—

CLEANTE. *(aside to MARIANNE)* Trust me. Just play along for a while. All will all be resolved.

(He brings her forward, pushing her against her will, to HARPAGON.)

CLEANTE. *(cont.)* This, father, is the delightful, incomparable Marianne.

(He brings her over to HARPAGON. She clings to CLEANTE.)

Look how she adores her new stepson already. *(aside)* Ugh! What a thought! *(to him)* Isn't she everything I said she would be?

MARIANNE. Stepson!?

(HARPAGON walks around her, inspecting from head to toe. He lifts her gown, peeks down the top of it, opens her mouth, and checks her teeth.)

HARPAGON. Well, well, well. No overstatement here. Very pleasing. Very pleasing.

(He coughs. MARIANNE is repulsed by his breath and turns away.)

HARPAGON. I am told you enjoy a phlegmy cough. You'll hear it often after we are married. What do you say to that!?

(He coughs again. She swoons.)

FROSINE!

(HARPAGON draws FROSINE aside.)

She doesn't like me. I get the distinct feeling she doesn't like me!

FROSINE. Oh monsieur, she is naturally timid and shy, and so overcome with powerful feelings of love for you, she can barely speak!

HARPAGON. Hmph.

(ELISE enters.)

Maybe my daughter can warm her up. Elise, come meet your new stepmother!

(The two women curtsy to each other. ELISE sees the look of terror on MARIANNE's face.)

ELISE. Forgive me for not being here the moment you arrived, to welcome you into our family. *(aside to her)* Don't fear, I understand a plot is unfolding to prevent this marriage and secure another much more amiable one.

MARIANNE. Oh, I hope so! No disrespect, but I just don't think I can bring myself to—to—

ELISE. You won't have to, I promise.

FROSINE. Oh look at that sweet sight. The stepmother and daughter bonding!

HARPAGON. *(to MAITRE SIMON, who is holding the bill under his nose)* Are you still here!?

MAITRE SIMON. Yes, and I am not leaving until you pay me!

HARPAGON. Then you'd better make yourself comfortable until I can send for the police to take you away!

MAITRE SIMON. No one could be comfortable in this miserable place.

HARPAGON. There's a perfectly fine chair right there.

MAITRE SIMON. I'm going to find a policeman and have you arrested!

HARPAGON By all means!

*(**MAITRE SIMON** exits.)*

Now, mademoiselle…what's her name?

CLEANTE. Marianne. May I take the liberty of telling you that my father has made such a brilliant choice that I must express my profound pleasure to you. I could not have chosen better myself. Why, I'm overjoyed at the prospect of you becoming my stepmother. It's almost too much to ask. I don't deserve such a fate.

MARIANNE. Neither do I. I feel exactly the same as you do. In fact, I am completely unworthy of the…honor he wishes to bestow upon me. *(to **HARPAGON**)* Excuse me a moment, sir. *(She takes **FROSINE** aside.)* Madame Frosine, this is a very peculiar position to be in! You didn't tell me he was so…old!

FROSINE. Well, now, dear, age is such a relative thing, isn't it? To a man of eighty, Monsieur Harpagon looks like the very picture of youth.

MARIANNE. Yes, well, think how he looks to a person of twenty!

FROSINE. Well, I admit he hasn't got the face you'd choose if things were different, or if you hadn't met the younger version.

MARIANNE. It's true and there's no point in denying it. It was love at first sight, the minute I saw… *(singing)* … My dear, sweet Cleante! *(speaking)* I'd rather have him than anybody else in the world, even if he weren't as handsome as he is. After all, his father has money, that's what you told me. Surely some of it will pass to his dear son, and then my poor, frail invalid mother would be well provided for?

FROSINE. *(aside)* Doesn't this break your heart!? You know, the old goat hasn't paid me yet, nor is he likely to. I'm very tempted to switch sides. *(to **HARPAGON**)* Well, monsieur, there she is. I leave it to you to woo her.

CLEANTE. *(jumping in)* Indeed, let us see some wooing of this precious young maid! For I must admit, my father could not have chosen better. Yes, you will be the most charming stepmother a young man could ask for. I can already imagine our nights together, sitting at table, enjoying a sumptuous dinner, laughing and talking, then sitting before the fire, my head resting in your lap, your soft, sweet hand caressing my tousled locks, me looking up into your adoring and adored face, and then we climb the stairs together, and you kiss me good night—

HARPAGON. How's that!?

CLEANTE. —On the forehead. Oh, I can picture it, like a Rembrandt painting, the candle casting a transcendent glow onto your beautiful, angelic face, the only light in the darkened hallway.

HARPAGON. Don't be offended by his nonsense, my girl!

MARIANNE. I assure you, monsieur, I am not the least offended. On the contrary, it has been very pleasurable to hear your son express his feelings so frankly. It speaks of a noble character and a sensitive imagination.

HARPAGON. Yes, well, he'll outgrow such foolery. It's kind of you to overlook his shortcomings.

MARIANNE. I hope he never outgrows them.

CLEANTE I never shall.

HARPAGON. I don't know where you get this streak of stubbornness! Must have been from your mother.

CLEANTE. My mother was the sweetest woman who ever lived—until now. But father, perhaps you'll let me speak for you, since you want me to change my tune, I will explain to this lovely creature the passion and the love you feel for her.

HARPAGON. I'm perfectly capable of speaking for myself!

CLEANTE. Yes, I can imagine vividly what you will say. You will say that she is the most charming person you have ever met, or could ever hope to meet, that your greatest happiness in life would be to be loved by her, that she is more precious to you than—than—gold, that the passion you feel for her shines like a brilliant diamond—like this huge diamond ring he wears on his crooked little finger! Is that not true, father?

HARPAGON. Diamond ring? More precious!?

CLEANTE. Yes! Because you are the diamond, dear— *(singing softly)* Marianne, Marianne, oh my dear Marianne— *(He tries to yank the ring from* **HARPAGON***'s hand, but it won't budge. He takes* **MARIANNE** *over and sticks his hand under her nose.)*

HARPAGON. What are you doing!? Give me back my hand!

CLEANTE. *(ignoring his father and dragging him and* **MARIANNE** *to the light)* You must look at it from a closer angle. In the light.

MARIANNE. Yes, it's quite nice. Very brilliant.

HARPAGON. Stop this! I want my hand back!

CLEANTE. *(holding his father's arm tightly and still trying to detach the ring)* He wants you to have it, as a present, a token of his tremendous esteem.

HARPAGON. WHAT!

CLEANTE. You do want her to have it, don't you, father?

HARPAGON. Are you joking!!??

CLEANTE. Remember, father, we are not a joking family.*(to* **MARIANNE***)* He means you must accept the present, or he will feel insulted, rejected.

MARIANNE. But, I have no desire—

CLEANTE. To hurt his feelings, do you?

HARPAGON. Hurt my feelings!? You're hurting my arm! What is going on here!?

MARIANNE. I couldn't possibly—

CLEANTE. Refuse such a kind offering.

HARPAGON. *(clutching his chest with the free hand)* What is he doing!? Oh! My heart!—

CLEANTE. You see? He says his heart will be broken if you don't accept it.

HARPAGON. My arm will be broken!

CLEANTE. He wants the world to know that you are his diamond.

MARIANNE I have no wish to—

CLEANTE. He wouldn't dream of taking it back—

HARPAGON. This is intolerable!

CLEANTE. You see? He says it would be intolerable of you to try and return it.

(Enter **MAITRE SIMON.***)*

MAITRE SIMON. You can never find a policeman when you need one! All right, Monsieur the miser, I am going to get my fee out of you or die trying!

(He pulls **HARPAGON** *from* **CLEANTE** *and backs him into a corner and starts rifling through his pockets.)*

HARPAGON. Stop that! You're tickling me! I'm very ticklish!

(He begins to laugh uncontrollably as **MAITRE SIMON** *searches him. Enter* **MAITRE JACQUES**, *who goes to* **HARPAGON**.*)*

MAITRE JACQUES. S'il vous plait, monsieur, I need more potatoes, and more butter! I 'ave only zees leetle beet left! Just a few ecus for to go and buy more! Please, on my knees I beg you!

(He sinks to his knees holding the butter as **HARPAGON** *continues laughing and* **MAITRE SIMON** *continues searching. They move around the room;* **MAITRE JACQUES** *follows them on his knees, still pleading.* **ELISE** *and* **MARIANNE** *follow* **HARPAGON**'s *flailing arm and admire the ring together.* **FROSINE** *approaches* **HARPAGON** *and* **SIMON**, *who are still grappling.)*

HARPAGON. *(laughing, yet very upset and agitated)* It's a plot—they all want to kill me! Get away from me—all of you!

FROSINE. On the off chance that you find money on him, he hasn't paid me either.

*(***FROSINE**, **MAITRE SIMON**, **HARPAGON**, *and* **MAITRE**

JACQUES *all start talking at once and loud. They continue through the next section between* **CLEANTE** *and* **LA FLECHE**, *who enters from the garden, covered in dirt, all his pockets bulging to the max, walking as if heavily laden with excess weight. He signals to* **CLEANTE**, *who edges over to him.*)

LA FLECHE. *(unable to speak from the excess weight he is carrying and his labor in the garden)* Psst!

CLEANTE. What!?

(**LA FLECHE** *mouths the words "I got the gold".* **CLEANTE** *does not hear over the noise of voices of the others.*)

Huh? I can't hear you!

(**LA FLECHE** *mouths the words again.* **CLEANTE** *shrugs his shoulders.* **LA FLECHE** *decides to do a charade.*)

Oh. A charade. I love charades. Four words. First word.

(**LA FLECHE** *points to his eye.*)

I? Good! Second word.

(**LA FLECHE** tugs on his own ear)

Sounds like…

(**LA FLECHE** *points his finger like a gun for "shot."*)

Rifle? Gun?

(**LA FLECHE** *tries "knot."*)

Bow? Knot?

(**LA FLECHE** *indicates yes.*)

Hmm. Sounds like knot. Bot, cot, clot, dot, fot, got—

(**LA FLECHE** *stops him, indicates yes.*)

Got! I got…

(**LA FLECHE** *holds up 3 fingers.*)

Third word. Small word.

(does the list rapidly)

In, on, and, but, or, nor, for, of, the—

(**LA FLECHE** *stops him.*)

The! Oh good! What's next?

(LA FLECHE, now exhausted, holds up 4 fingers.)

CLEANTE. *(cont.)* Fourth word. Fingers? Hand?

(LA FLECHE takes a gold coin from one of the pockets and holds it up.)

Coin?

(LA FLECHE holds up another one, then shows his bulging pockets.)

Money? GOLD!?

(LA FLECHE puts his hand over CLEANTE's mouth. CLEANTE speaks muffled.)

You got the gold!

(LA FLECHE takes a clump of coins from one of his pockets and gives some to CLEANTE, who goes over to MAITRE SIMON, who now has HARPAGON on the floor, exhausted from laughing. CLEANTE taps MAITRE SIMON on the shoulder, hands him a few coins. MAITRE SIMON takes them and runs out. Then CLEANTE turns to MAITRE JACQUES, who is still pleading with HARPAGON for money to buy food for the dinner.)

Here! Go and buy more potatoes. And a suckling pig, and six chickens, and paté and a goose and all the butter you can carry! Oh, and get hay for those poor horses!

HARPAGON. *(still on the floor, exhausted and panting)* Gold!? Do I see gold!? What's he doing with all those gold pieces!? Did he find my secret–

MAITRE JACQUES. Oh, monsieur Cleante! Merci mille fois! I am a 'appy man!

(He starts to run out, drops a coin. HARPAGON sees it, and they both dive for it and wrestle during the following exchange between FROSINE and LA FLECHE. MAITRE JACQUES wins the coin battle and starts to rush out the door. CLEANTE stops him and grabs the butter, and MAITRE JACQUES exits as LA FLECHE, still barely able to move, signals to FROSINE, who approaches him. LA

FLECHE *hands a few coins to* **FROSINE**. *She grabs them and takes him aside.)*

FROSINE. I have a plan to help the young lovers out of their mess, but I need your help.

LA FLECHE. *(gasping for air)* Only if it teaches the old man a lesson.

FROSINE. Let's say it has the potential. Now, here's what we're going to do…

(She whispers to **LA FLECHE**. *He nods.)*

And then…

(She whispers again. **LA FLECHE** *smiles broadly and nods again.)*

You secure the gold somewhere safe and come back later, as per my instructions, and we'll see what will be.

*(***LA FLECHE** *staggers out.* **CLEANTE** *crosses to* **HARPAGON**, *spreads the butter on his finger, and finally jerks the ring off.)*

HARPAGON. Ow! What was that!?

*(***CLEANTE** *rushes to* **MARIANNE**.*)*

CLEANTE. Here. We're engaged!

(Appropriate oohing and aahing from **MARIANNE** *and* **ELISE**. **VALERE** *enters with* **MAITRE SIMON**, *carrying a sofa.* **MAITRE SIMON** *is now playing* **FURNITURE MOVER**. *Yes, the fastest costume change in theatre history.)*

VALERE. Monsieur, there are some men outside with a bunch of furniture. Should I let them in?

HARPAGON. What!? No! Who ordered furniture!?

CLEANTE. I did!

HARPAGON. *(finally getting to his feet and crossing to the sofa, out of breath)* I won't have it in here! Oh God! All the neighbors watching this ornate Louis Quinze bilge being delivered—they'll know what I've got, they'll know and they'll come looking, crawling all over this place…put that down!

VALERE. Very well.

*(**VALERE** lets his end of the couch drop on **HARPAGON**'s foot.)*

HARPAGON. Ow! Ow! Ow! My foot!

(He hops around, holding his foot, and ends up on the couch, crying and gasping for air.)

CLEANTE. We're going to have a beautiful salon once again—and a magnificent wedding!

MARIANNE. Wonderful!

ELISE. How exciting!

HARPAGON. *(a disheveled wreck)* What is going on here!? People attacking me from all sides, tickling me, servants disobeying, fancy furniture, gold being thrown all over the place, and—and—and— *(He looks at his ring hand.)* I lost my diamond ring!

(blackout)

END OF ACT I

ACT II

SCENE ONE

(The same room, now elegantly and sumptuously furnished. Chairs, sofas, paintings on the walls, drapes, etc. ELISE, VALERE, MARIANNE, and CLEANTE sit around on the new furniture. Long silence. Periodically they get up and move to a different piece.)

MARIANNE. This one is very comfortable.

ELISE. So is this.

CLEANTE. I'm not crazy about this one.

(long pause)

ELISE. How long do you suppose before he finds out we're a bunch of thieves?

VALERE. Not long now.

ELISE. What were we thinking!?

MARIANNE. What's the use of having his gold? If we touch it, we're thieves, and I still have to marry the man my mother arranged for me to marry. I can't go against her wishes. She's...

ALL. A poor frail invalid.

*(**MAITRE JACQUES** enters from the front door with a bunch of dead chickens and a goose over his shoulder, singing joyously He crosses and exits to the kitchen area.)*

CLEANTE. Well, at least we'll have a sumptuous feast tonight.

ELISE. Why won't he tell anybody where he hid the gold? He's being very stubborn.

VALERE. No, loyal. If he's the only thief, he'll go to prison and not us.

CLEANTE. And we can all honestly say we haven't seen the cashbox and don't know where it is.

MARIANNE. Oh, how clever!

CLEANTE. The biggest problem is keeping father out of the garden, so he won't find out his money's gone. Of course, we can't keep him in the dark forever.

*(**MAITRE JACQUES** crosses back to the front door and exits.)*

MARIANNE. Where is your father?

VALERE. He went out to find a policeman to arrest Maitre Simon for attacking him.

ELISE. This was a very bad idea. We can't use the money to run away—we'll be fugitives our whole lives!

CLEANTE. Father wouldn't put us in prison! Would he?

VALERE. Speculation won't help us right now. We have to plan, strategize. The most important thing is to keep your father in this room. And the best way to do that is to start an argument with him.

MARIANNE. Oh, you are all so smart and clever and nice, I do hope I can become a part of your family…except if I have to—have to—

*(She cries. Everyone comforts her. **MAITRE JACQUES** re-enters with a suckling pig, crosses into the kitchen.)*

VALERE. Don't worry, everybody. Everything is going to work out just fine.

ELISE. How do you know that? You can't possibly make a sweeping generality like that. It has no foundation!

VALERE. Are you doubting my word?

ELISE. I'm doubting the logic of it.

VALERE. Well, perhaps, then, you're doubting everything about me.

ELISE. I didn't say that!

VALERE. It certainly sounded like that to me.

ELISE. Well, then, perhaps I am doubting everything about you! You're always right, so you must be right about that, too!

VALERE. I'm always right? Talk about sweeping generalizations! Oh, listen to us. We're at each other's throats, and all because of money.

*(*CLEANTE *and* MARIANNE *look at them.* CLEANTE *is about to speak, when* MAITRE JACQUES *crosses again to the front door and exits. They wait until he leaves.)*

ELISE. I wonder if Señor Anselme makes sweeping generalizations?

VALERE. Oh really? Well, I know a good way of finding out!

ELISE. Oh, really? What would that be?

VALERE. Why, marry him, of course!

ELISE. Oh! Well, perhaps I should. They say you only get to know someone after you're married, not before. I think they may be right.

VALERE. Is that what they say? I'm beginning to think they're right, too.

ELISE. Yes, I believe they are. I certainly would never have supposed you to be the kind of person who ignores an engagement and suggests to his fiancée that she marry someone else!

VALERE. And I would never have supposed that my fiancée would be so willing to ignore her engagement and consider marrying someone else just to find out if he makes generalizations or not!

ELISE. I can see that our love was a pitiful illusion!

VALERE. It certainly appears that way! I thought you were wise and sensible.

ELISE. You thought I was a mermaid!

VALERE. And you thought I was some sort of Sir Galahad, in full armor, ready to save you from all perils and keep you from life's troubles forever!

ELISE. Frankly, I can't believe I was ever in love with you!

VALERE. Frankly, I can't believe you ever were either!

CLEANTE. Wait a minute! *(to* ELISE*)* Engaged? You two!? In love?

MARIANNE. People fight like that when they're in love!?

CLEANTE. Not us, my sweetest buttercup. Never us. But it certainly sounds like *they* are!

ELISE. Correction, we were.

VALERE. Correction: we are. Darling, look at us, quarreling over nothing. This is what living under the influence of an obsessive man can do to people. I'm sorry.

ELISE. I'm sorry too!

CLEANTE. Hold on a minute! I want to know what's going on between you two.

ELISE. Well, you might as well, for all the good it will do us now. Yes, my dear brother, Valere and I are in love.

CLEANTE. How long has this been going on!?

ELISE. Since he came here to be father's valet.

VALERE. Since before that. Since I first laid eyes on her.

ELISE. Under water.

VALERE. During a shipwreck.

CLEANTE. Well, I'm breaking it off, because I won't have it! He's a—he's-a servant!

ELISE. No, he's not. He's…traveling in disguise, until he can find his long lost noble family from…where was it?

VALERE. San Burgos de La Extremadura Cathtella Villa Nueva del Cordoba—

(MAITRE JACQUES re-enters with a bale of hay and crosses to the other side. Shortly we hear the sound of horses neighing excitedly.)

—Tacarimba de Almadóvar. Near Barthelona.

ELISE. That's it. He's from there. At least that's what he says. I don't know what to believe any more.

CLEANTE. But how did you come to lose your family?

VALERE. Shipwreck.

CLEANTE. That seems to be a recurring theme in your life.

VALERE. You could say that.

(The doorbell rings.)

ALL. Oh!

ELISE. Someone's at the door!

CLEANTE Does father know already!?

ELISE. Could it be the police!?

MARIANNE. What should we do?

(The bell again.)

VALERE. Someone has to go and see who it is.

(He exits while the rest stand or sit frozen in fear. Enter **FROSINE** *and* **VALERE**. **FROSINE** *is in disguise as Mme. Poquelin, wig, tasteless gown, warts and fake nose. She carries a large cashbox. No one recognizes her)*

Madame Poquelin, ladies and gentlemen.

CLEANTE. Oh God , no!

FROSINE. *(speaking with a lisp)* Bonjour, tout le monde! Where ith my fianthé? I cannot thtand another moment without theeing him!

CLEANTE. *(averting his eyes, speaking to* **ELISE***)* Tell me, is it as bad as I think?

ELISE. You couldn't imagine worse in a million years.

FROSINE. There he ith—I'd know him anywhere! Oh my dear, thweet boy, I remember you when you romped in my yard at the age of –what—theven?

CLEANTE. *(slowly, painfully turning his head to look at her)* Oh yes, and I remember you.

FROSINE. When Frothine thent me that beautiful note from your father, I wath thwept away and came potht-hathte! Well, aren't you going to kith your bride-to-be?

ELISE. *(aside, with a giggle)* If you can find a place on her cheek where there isn't a hairy wart or a pockmark.

CLEANTE. I fail to see the humor in this.

(He closes his eyes and kisses her lightly on the cheek. She grabs him and plants a big one on his mouth.)

FROSINE. Now that'th a kith!

CLEANTE. *(turning away and wiping his mouth with a handkerchief)* Yeth, that definitely wath—was.

MARIANNE. This is your fiancée!? I—I—I—didn't know you had become engaged.

CLEANTE. *(aside to her)* I haven't and she isn't. It's all my father's idea. She has a lot of money.

VALERE. May I take your wrap, madame? And your…box?

FROSINE. Oh, not my bokth! I never let my bokth out of my thight! It'th full of gold, you know. I have a ton of gold. And I love to uthe it to help people in thorny thituationth.

ELISE. Wonderful. Someone who could help us out of our mess, and we can't tell her.

FROSINE. Of courth you can! Your mother and I were the clothetht of freindth. There ith nothing I would not do for her offthpring if they were in trouble.

MARIANNE. Do we dare?

ELISE. Could we try?

CLEANTE. Can we trust?

VALERE. *(looking closely at her and guessing her identity)* You know, I think this very kind lady will be completely trustworthy and join our camp.

FROSINE. Thmart lad. You are abtholutely correct. Let'th go—thpill it out.

ELISE. Well, you see…

VALERE. The situation is.…

CLEANTE. Where do we start?

MARIANNE *(suddenly finding her spine, speaking very fast)* Your fiancé Cleante and I are in love and we want to get married, and his sister Elise and this nice young man, who you think is a valet but is really from a noble family from San Burgos de La Extremadura Cathtella Villa Nueva del Cordoba Tacarimba de Almadóvar, near Barthelona, want to get married as well, but their father, who has decided to marry me because I'm poor and won't expect fancy dresses and hats and jewels and go out gambling and such and will therefore be more economical, has all the money and refuses to listen to either of his children or their aching hearts, but has arranged marriages with you for her son and a Señor Anselme for his daughter, the former because you're wealthy and he thinks you will pay him so you can have a handsome young stud to ride your saddle, and the latter because he will take her without a dowry. That's it in a nutshell. Oh, through Cleante's servant, we also stole his cashbox, but we don't know where it is because Cleante's servant won't tell us and we can't use it to run away anyway because I have to obey my poor, frail invalid mother's wishes and because her father would no doubt have us arrested and put in prison anyway, so you find us in dire straits.

FROSINE. Oh, you poor, dear little moppeth! Why, I had no idea! I would never think of marrying thomeone jutht to be able to hop in the thack with him! And what could your father be thinking about?

ALL. Money.

FROSINE. Oh yeth, well everyone'th thinking and worrying about money thethe *(these)* dayth. But, I think I can perthuade him to change hith mind about ethpouthing thith lovely young lady and turn hith amorouth feelingth elthewhere. *(finally in her own voice)* What do you think, Monthieur Cleante? Am I up to the tathk?

CLEANTE. *(peering at her closely)* Sacre bleu! It's Frosine!

(general mayhem and delight from everyone)

FROSINE. You just leave everything to Madame Frosine. I haven't been a marriage broker for twenty years for naught.

ELISE. What are you planning to do!?

FROSINE. Convince him to turn away from Marianne and marry me! I've got a cashbox equal to his own, and then some. Money talkth, my thweet.

CLEANTE. But where did you suddenly come up with all this money?

FROSINE. I… skipped on lunches.

VALERE. Do you really want to marry him!?

FROSINE. Oh, we'll worry about that later. The important thing is to get the young lovers married. The rest will take care of itself. Now, where is he?

CLEANTE. Out looking for a policeman.

FROSINE. Well, that could take a while. There have been so many cutbacks on our protective forces since this—

ALL. Economic downturn.

VALERE. And we have to keep him in this room as long as possible, so he doesn't discover his gold is missing until we get him to change his mind about the marriages.

FROSINE. All right, we sit and wait.

(They sit down. A long pause, then enter **MAITRE JACQUES.***)*

MAITRE JACQUES. Oh, mon Dieu, ze deener guests 'ave arrived! But, le grand Maitre Jacques, chef extraordinaire, is all prepared!

(He exits, and returns immediately with a tray of hors-d'oeuvres.)

A leetle sample of ze grand fete to come.

(He sets the tray of hors-d'oeuvres on a table. They all begin munching, **MAITRE JACQUES** *exits and returns with a split of champagne on a rolling cart containing champagne flutes. He proceeds to open the bottle.)*

CLEANTE. Oh, paté! Oh, have you ever tasted such a flavor!?

(enthusiastic mms, oohs and aahs from the ensemble)

ELISE. I can't remember when I've eaten anything so delicious in this house!

VALERE. Champagne! *(He tastes.)* Veuve Cliquot, 1632. That was a good year.

MARIANNE. And shrimp! Oh, I must get the recipe!

MAITRE JACQUES. Maitre Jacques never geeves away ees secrets!

ELISE. I confess, I was getting very tired of vegetable soup.

(A door slams offstage. They all freeze.)

HARPAGON. *(from offstage)* Aargh, you can never find a policeman when you need one!

(Everyone begins stuffing their mouths with the remaining hors d'oeuvres, **MAITRE JACQUES** *quickly wheels the champagne cart out of the room, the tray goes under the sofa cushions, and they all compose themselves as* **HARPAGON** *enters, eying them suspiciously.)*

What's going on in here!? I told you to get rid of all this fancy frippery! The whole neighborhood will be at our door asking for handouts! And just how were you able to afford such—such—opulence!?

CLEANTE. *(with his mouth full)* I won at cards, father. I rented it for our special guests. We're all just getting acquainted.

VALERE. *(swallowing hard)* Monsieur, Mme. Poquelin has arrived.

HARPAGON. Oh? That was quick!

FROSINE. *(rising to greet him with her Mme. Poquelin voice, spitting her wad of food into a small purse she is carrying)* Oh yeth, monsieur! The theckond I retheived your note from that kind Mme. Frothine, I dropped everything and thcurried over here. What a delight to thee you again, after tho many yearth! And you don't look a day older!

HARPAGON. *(looking at her with absolute horror)* Yes, well, people have been telling me that. And you…look exactly the same as well.

FROSINE. Oh, you do know how to pleathe a woman, don't you!?

HARPAGON. I hope my lovely bride-to-be thinks so, eh?

FROSINE. And I hope your thon hath the thame charm ath hith father!

ELISE. *(finishing up her wad of paté)* Father, perhaps we should offer our guests something to drink.

HARPAGON. Yes, of course. Would anyone like a nice cool glass of water? Maitre Jacques! MAITRE JACQUES!

MAITRE JACQUES. *(Each time he enters, his apron and his face get dirtier.)* Oui, monsieur!?

HARPAGON. Water for everyone!

MAITRE JACQUES. Water?

HARPAGON. Water.

MAITRE JACQUES. But we 'ave—

VALERE. *(rushing up to him)* No time to lose. Water, Jacques.

MAITRE JACQUES. But ze cham—

VALERE. –pion chef is going to fetch some water. *(aside to him)* Monsieur doesn't know about the champagne. Shh!

MAITRE JACQUES. Ah. Ze 'ard times, once again. I weel 'ide ze you-know-what.

HARPAGON. And while we're waiting, I'm going to check on the—ah—worms in the garden.

ALL. NO!

VALERE. It's impolite to leave your guests for worms, monsieur.

HARPAGON. What do I care? They're here to sign contracts. It's a business meeting.

VALERE. I beg to disagree, sir. They are here to discuss their future lives, and you are the person responsible for every transaction that will take place in this room.

HARPAGON. Well, they have the rest of their lives to honor their contracts, so a few minutes more isn't going to make a difference.

VALERE. Oh, but it will, monsieur, it will!

HARPAGON. What's the matter with you, all of a sudden!? You never disagree with me.

VALERE. Well, up to now, you've always been right. But I strongly believe that you need to stay right here and supervise the discussion of the three marriage contracts. *(aside to others)* Help me out, here! Start an argument!

CLEANTE. Father, I refuse to marry Mme. Poquelin.

ELISE. And I don't want to marry Señor Anselme!

FROSINE. And I abtholutely will not marry your thon!

MARIANNE. And I really don't want to marry you, monsieur.

VALERE. So you see, we are a long way off from any agreement on any of these contracts, and we need you in the room to—uh—negotiate.

HARPAGON. What sort of revolt is this!?

CLEANTE. A revolt of the heart! Passion and love drive us to say and do these things!

ELISE. We're miserable, father!

(**MARIANNE** *starts crying,* **ELISE** *joins her, the men comfort their sweethearts, and* **FROSINE** *zeroes in on* **HARPAGON**.)

FROSINE. Oh, now, monthieur Harpagon, I remember thothe dayth tho long ago, when I would vithit your dear, wife, before she pathed away, and she would dethcribe you ath the kindetht, motht conthiderate man she'd ever known! Indeed, I remember you that way, how tender you were with her, and with your dear little children!

HARPAGON. Hmph. I don't remember it.

FROSINE. Ah, it'th alwayth the kind, generouth oneth who don't realithe their own value. In fact, monthieur, if you would know the truth, I would tho much prefer to marry you mythelf.

HARPAGON. *(horrified)* Yourthelf!? I mean, the die is cast. *Les jeux sont faits*, the contracts are about to be drawn up with the names on them. I've sent for a marriage broker–he'll be here any minute!

(doorbell)

You see? There he is! *(aside)* Thank God.

FROSINE. *(opening her own cashbox and flashing the gold)* Are you abtholutely thertain?

HARPAGON. *(drawn to the box like a fly to honey)* What was that?

(She flashes it again, leaving the box open a little longer. He starts to reach his hand into it, and she slams it shut. Doorbell again.)

HARPAGON. Hold that thought.

(He exits.)

VALERE. We can't keep him in here much longer.

ELISE. He'll have to go to the cashbox to pay the marriage broker!

CLEANTE. Perhaps…but Frosine has gold to pay him. Of course we'd pay you back.

FROSINE. Oh, I don't think it will come to that.

*(Enter **HARPAGON** with the marriage broker, who is **LA FLECHE**, in disguise. Everyone recognizes him except **HARPAGON**. **LA FLECHE** speaks with a German accent)*

FROSINE. Ah, the marriage broker hath arrived! And I believe I know him! *(aside, to **LA FLECHE**)* Stall as long as possible!

LA FLECHE. Jah, meine frau! I am Herr Otto von Meerschmurtz, of Pfaffenhoffen, Gotterdammerung, Wurtennberg, Meerschmurtz und Katz.

FROSINE. Yeth, I thought I recognithed you! I believe you drew up the paperth for my thecond, or wath it my third marriage?

HARPAGON. I didn't know you had married more than once.

FROSINE. Oh yeth, dear monthieur. Three marriageth, three huthbandth dead.

HARPAGON. How unfortunate.

FROSINE. I wouldn't thay that. Each of them had a thizable fortune and no offthpring, tho all the money from all three ethtates went to me! *(She opens the cashbox again.)*

HARPAGON. *(peeking in and staring at the gold)* How—how—how much have you amassed?

FROSINE. You know, thereth tho much in there, I have no idea! I can't count up that far.

HARPAGON. *(aside)* She's never going to hand all that over just to marry my son. Perhaps I should reconsider... *(He looks at her face.)* No.

LA FLECHE. Javol. Unt now I am here to draw up das contracts for tree more, iss dis not correct, Herr Harpagon?

HARPAGON. Jah—yes. Mme. Frosine sent you over to me per my instructions.

LA FLECHE. Jah—vat a vonderful voman. I vould luff to get meine hands on zat von!

HARPAGON. Yes, well, very good. Have a seat, I'll be right back. I need to go the garden for a moment.

CLEANTE, ELISE, VALERE, MARIANNE, FROSINE. NO!

LA FLECHE. Herr Harpagon, you vant to leaf me here mit das clock ticking, tick-tock, tick-tock, unt my fee iss piling up for each second zat you keep me vaiting!?

HARPAGON. You charge by the hour?

LA FLECHE. I charge by ze minute! Zometimes by ze second! Durink zese troubled times, many many people are getting married, because, I'm sure you know, two can liff cheaper den von. Unt zo, many people who should never, never liff in das connubial bliss, are making das marriage vows. I am a busy busy man, unt I don't haff time to vait because you vant to go sniff das roses in das garden.

HARPAGON. I'll be right back—I just have to check on— the worms.

(He starts for the garden door. Everyone waits in frozen fear.)

LA FLECHE. Vell, you can go look at your vorms, or you can write up ze marriage papers. I have einz, zvie, drei, fier more contracts to write after zese, before die ent of diss day; I sink I must leaf. Unt, if I leaf, good luck finding zomeone else to come to your house!

HARPAGON. All right, all right, have a seat at the desk and we'll begin.

LA FLECHE. Javol. You are a shmart man, mein herr.

*(**LA FLECHE** takes out a cloth, wipes down the chair and the desk, takes out his quill, bottle of ink, papers, slowly, elaborately, in a long, drawn-out ceremony; settles himself into the chair, squirms a bit, gets up, goes to a pillow on the sofa, brings it back, plumps it up, smooths it out, puts it on the stool, and settles himself down.)*

HARPAGON. I thought you were in a hurry!

LA FLECHE. Zat iss exactly vy zere iss no time to vaste! To write a perfect, beautiful, contract iss a very difficult sing to do! Each von takes time! I cannot be rushed, mein herr.

HARPAGON. He'll drive me mad!

LA FLECHE. Now, contract number von. *(He dips the pen in the bottle, and proceeds to write "contract #1" as he repeats the words aloud. Then he pauses and thinks.)* Vereas, in accordance mit das laws regarding marriage on zis—nein nein. Zat's ze vay I always begin my contracts. I'm tired of zis phrase. I make somesink better.

*(He ruminates. **HARPAGON** watches him until he can't take it another second.)*

HARPAGON. I don't care what sentence, or phrase or word you begin it with, just get the names down!

LA FLECHE. You vant das names, right avay? Ludvig iss going to marry Helga?

HARPAGON. There is no Ludwig and there is certainly no Helga! I want a paper that says my son Cleante is going to marry Mme. Poquelin, my daughter Elise is going to marry Señor Anselme, and I am going to marry Mlle. Marianne! And Valere, you'll be the witness.

LA FLECHE. Jah, jah, von moment, you are speaking too kvickly. *(He writes as he speaks.)* Herr Cleante vill marry Fraulein Marianne, Fraulein Elise vill marry Herr Valere, unt Herr Harpagon vill marry Frau Poquelin, mit Herr Anselme as vitness.

HARPAGON. No, no, no! you've got it all twisted up!

(dragging the couples over and pairing them up, getting confused himself in the process)

HARPAGON. *(cont.)* My son is marrying this girl, my daughter is marrying what's his name—Valere, you stand in for Señor Anselme, and I am marrying this young lady.

(Everyone shifts around so they end up with their chosen mates.)

LA FLECHE. You are marrying zis sveet young fraulein! Oh, zat's a good von! Oh jah, I luff a good joke! But uff course you are making mit a joke! *(He looks at* **HARPAGON***'s face.)* Oh. Diss iss not a joke. Uh-oh, I make ze social gaffe, jah? All right. Now, let me zee… *(confusing everybody)* Ziss young fraulein iss Marianne, ziss young fraulein iss Elise, das is Señor Anselme, unt diss iss your son Cleante.

HARPAGON. You are an incompetent, maddening, worthless ninny!

(A dog barks again. Everyone freezes.)

ALL. The dog!

HARPAGON. The dog! The damn dog is back! He's going to dig up my—onions!

(He rushes into the garden. Everybody clears the stage in a nanosecond, running in all directions. There is a long pause, we see some dirt fly up and then–)

Stop, thief! Stop, thief! Stop, thief! Assassin! Murderer! I've been assassinated, that's what's happened. My throat's been cut. My fortune is gone. Somebody took it!

(re-entering from the garden)

Who did it? Who did it? Who left me with an empty hole in the ground? DIRT! I'm left with nothing but dirt! Where is he? He's hiding. I must find him. But which way should I go? Here! No here! There. Oh, my mind is not working well. Wait! What happened to everybody!? All right, where am I? I'm…here. It looks

HARPAGON.(*cont.*) familiar. My salon? Of course. Everything looks the same, except for one thing. THE GOLD IS GONE!!! That's it, I'm a dead man. I'm burned as toast. History.

Oh, my poor, poor gold, my helpmeet, my companion, my friend! My support, my consolation, my joy. They took you away. All away. Far away from me. And they won't bring you back. Why won't they bring you back? I want them to bring you back. GIVE ME BACK MY MONEY!!! Nobody took it. It just disappeared. God took it. A divine practical joke. God does things like this sometimes. That must be it. No, Nobody took it. Or somebody took it. Let me think. Carefully. Methodically. Now, where was I when it disappeared? I was…talking to that idiot marriage broker. Aha! He's an accomplice. He was sent to distract me so the thief could get in and get it. Oh, and I fell for it and now I'll never trust anyone again. Not friends, not strangers, certainly not my children. No one. No one I've ever known or seen. Oh, God, swarms of faces swim before me and not one of them can I trust.

(*picking two people in the audience, perhaps coming down into the audience*)

Look at those two, whispering to each other. About the robbery, of course. Maybe one of them knows who did it. Listen, if you know anything, or think you know anything, no matter how insignificant it may seem, tell me. Please! Did someone strange sit next to you in the last ten minutes? Is there a police detective in the house? I've been robbed! Does no one care? This is a heinous crime! The perpetrator deserves the rope! No, that's too humane. He deserves to suffer. The rack first. No, even that's too quick and too easy. He can lie down through it. I want him to suffer. I want him to scream in agony. Hot oil poured all over him, poison to make him cry out to be killed, then have him drawn and quartered, and only then—the axe. That's it. You have to walk up the steps, you have to kneel, no lying down, no laziness when you get the axe. That's it. I want to see a beheading. His head on a stick if we find him. Mine if we don't!

(He falls to the floor, sobbing. Blackout.)

SCENE TWO

*(When the lights come up, **HARPAGON** is sitting on one of the chairs, sobbing into a handkerchief. **INSPECTOR SANSCLOU** is looking around the room for clues. He is the original Inspector Clouseau. **MARIANNE**, **CLEANTE**, **FROSINE**, **VALERE**, **ELISE LA FLECHE**, and **MAITRE JACQUES** stand, huddled together, awaiting their fates.)*

INSPECTOR SANSCLOU. Your name, monsieur?

HARPAGON. *(through his sobs)* Har-harp—Harpagon!

*(**SANSCLOU** settles in at the desk.)*

Have you found anything? Anything at all?

INSPECTOR SANSCLOU. Nothing yet. This burglar was clearly a professional. But nothing will prevent me from discovering the miserable, wretched brigand thief who delivered you into such... misery. I am an artiste when it comes to solving a crime. No thief, murderer, or charlatan escapes my clutches. It's who I am and what I do. You have nothing to worry about. *(Taking out a little notebook, and dipping the quill pen, he writes everything **HARPAGON** tells him.)* Now, who lives here besides yourself?

HARPAGON. My son, my daughter, my servant, my cook—

INSPECTOR SANSCLOU. Cook...

MAITRE JACQUES. Chef–

HARPAGON. And my son has a valet. I've never trusted the fellow. Shifty eyes.

INSPECTOR SANSCLOU. Aha! Shifty eyes. That could be a clue. Did anyone else come to the house today?

HARPAGON. A young lady—my fiancée. Mlle. Marianne. That one, over there.

*(He points to her. She curtsies. **INSPECTOR SANSCLOU** gets up with his magnifying glass, goes over, and looks closely at her, particularly her cleavage.)*

Lives down the street. Too young and innocent to perpetrate such a crime. And no motivation. She was about to marry me.

INSPECTOR SANSCLOU. Marry you!? That's motivation enough! Perhaps she wanted your fortune the easy way?

HARPAGON. She does have a poor, frail, invalid mother…

CLEANTE. It is impossible. This young lady had nothing to do with this case. She is an innocent bystander.

INSPECTOR SANSCLOU. No one is above suspicion in a case like this! *(writing)* Mademoiselle Marianne, lives down the street, poor invalid mother…

HARPAGON. Frail. You left out frail. Ah! There was a money lender named Simon. He attacked me!

INSPECTOR SANSCLOU. Aha! Attacked him…where is he?

VALERE. I don't think we'll be seeing any more of him.

INSPECTOR SANSCLOU. Aha! On the run. Very very suspicious. Now, how much gold did you have in your cashbox?

HARPAGON. Fifty thousand.

ALL. FIFTY THOUSAND!!??

CLEANTE. And we've been starving in this rat hole, eating nothing but vegetable soup!?

INSPECTOR SANSCLOU. And who are you?

HARPAGON. That's my son. He's too much of a booby to execute such a professional job.

INSPECTOR SANSCLOU. *(examining* **CLEANTE***)* Booby… *(eying* **MAITRE JACQUES***)* And you are?

MAITRE JACQUES. I am Maitre Jacques, ze chef extraordinaire.

INSPECTOR SANSCLOU. And where were you when the crime was being committed?

MAITRE JACQUES. In ze kitchen, preparing ze coq au vin and ze soufflé au fromage.

INSPECTOR SANSCLOU. Coq au vin!? Aha!

MAITRE JACQUES. Aha?

INSPECTOR SANSCLOU. Do you use cabernet or pinot for the sauce?

MAITRE JACQUES. Monsieur! Maitre Jacques does not reveal 'is trade secrets!

INSPECTOR SANSCLOU. I've always found that equal parts of both give it a most distinctive flavor. Have you ever tried that?

MAITRE JACQUES. Non! But, eet ees an interesting idea.

INSPECTOR SANSCLOU. And you know the choice of onion is very important.

MAITRE JACQUES. Oh, well, everyone knows zat! What do you use? Shallots? Valencias?

HARPAGON. Onions!? What does that have to do with the crime?

INSPECTOR SANSCLOU. Monsieur Har—harp—Harpagon, everything is a clue. For example, if he were not a real chef, if he were an imposteur, he would have given away his secret recipe for the coq au vin sauce. BUT! Do not think this rules you out, Maitre le chef extraordinaire. Everyone is suspect until I say they are not! *(He turns to* **CLEANTE.***)* Hmm. The son who likes to dress well. Who likes the finer things in life. Has he been spending money lately?

HARPAGON. He rented all this furniture.

INSPECTOR SANSCLOU. Aha! *(writing)* Rented furniture on the day of the crime! Very interesting.

CLEANTE. I won at the casino.

INSPECTOR SANSCLOU. Hmm. Possible gambling debts. *(He arrives at* **FROSINE***, warts and all, and screams.)* Who is this!?

HARPAGON. My son's fiancée, Mme. Poquelin.

INSPECTOR SANSCLOU. *(writing)* Aha. Even more suspicious! Son has bizarre taste in women…

CLEANTE. I do not! This is the woman I want to marry!

INSPECTOR SANSCLOU. Well, the plot thickens. So, son has motive for stealing gold. Loves his father's fiancée, if father is broke and he has the money, he can marry the little cabbage. *(in his face)* What do you have to say for yourself?

CLEANTE. I do not know where my father's cashbox is, and that's the truth.

INSPECTOR SANSCLOU. We'll see about that. We'll just see about that! *(noticing* **FROSINE**'s *cashbox)* Just a moment—what's that!?

FROSINE. It'th my cashbokth, and obviouthly it'th not mithing!

INSPECTOR SANSCLOU. Suspicious. Very suspicious. What's in it?

FROSINE. None of your buthiness.

INSPECTOR SANSCLOU. I must insist you open it. *(She flashes it like before.)* Packed with gold! How did a woman with that face come to possess so much gold?

FROSINE. Three dead huthbandth, Inthpector. How elthe do you think?

INSPECTOR SANSCLOU. If I were not so busy on this very difficult case, I would have to ask you how each of them died. But, that's another story. *(looking very carefully at everyone with his magnifier)* There's clearly some sort of cover-up going on here. I suspect…everyone! You and you, and you and you, you all look guilty to me! *(He settles on* **LA FLECHE.***)* And who is this!?

HARPAGON. My son's valet, La Fleche. I've never trusted him.

LA FLECHE. *(laying it on thick)* Oh yes, it was me! I stole the— what was it? I stole it, I stole it! I'm the one! it must be me! What did I do? What's my name? Where am I? Will they send me back to the asylum? I don't want to go to the asylum! *(hanging on to* **INSPECTOR SANSCLOU***)* You won't send me back to the asylum, will you?

INSPECTOR SANSCLOU. We can eliminate him. Too crazy to have done it. *(arrives at* **VALERE***)* Aha. Valere, the valet. How long have you been in your master's service?

HARPAGON. One month.

INSPECTOR SANSCLOU. One month!? And where were you employed before that?

VALERE. Elsewhere.

INSPECTOR SANSCLOU. And what are your references?

VALERE. I have none.

INSPECTOR SANSCLOU. No references? *(to* **HARPAGON***)* And you, Monsieur Har-Harp-Harpagon, engaged him without a single recommendation?

HARPAGON. He seemed trustworthy. He saved my daughter's life in a shipwreck. That seemed enough at the time.

INSPECTOR SANSCLOU. Admirable. Very admirable. But perhaps, monsieur Valere, you saw this beautiful, obviously rich and very charming young lady and pushed her overboard so you could save her and be the hero to her poor, distraught father!

ELISE. No! I was thrown from the ship by waves! He jumped in and saved me! He's the noblest, bravest, most dear and wonderful man anyone could ever hope to know!

CLEANTE. Isn't that nice? We're all in love.

VALERE. We certainly are!

ELISE. Completely!

HARPAGON. What's this!?

VALERE. We're engaged.

HARPAGON. Oh no, you're not!

INSPECTOR SANSCLOU. Aha! Two more lovers with a motive to steal. A definite conspiracy!

ELISE. A conspiracy to marry the people we love, you mean!

(instant protesting from everyone, building until they are all shouting at once, **HARPAGON** *wailing and sobbing, then–)*

HARPAGON. Don't listen to them—I have selected the grooms and brides, and there will be no changes—you hear me? No changes whatsoever!

(All prospective spouses start arguing at once with **HARPAGON** *until–)*

ANSELME. *(standing at the front door entrance)* Is this an inopportune moment?

(Everyone shuts up and looks at him.)

Have I arrived for dinner too early? Too late?

INSPECTOR SANSCLOU. And who is this?

HARPAGON. Señor Anselme. He is to be engaged to my daughter tonight.

INSPECTOR SANSCLOU. Aha! Returning to the scene of the crime!

ANSELME. Ridiculous! I've never set foot in this house before tonight! What crime am I accused of?

INSPECTOR SANSCLOU. Pilfering this worthy man's cashbox.

ANSELME. Nonsense. I have plenty of my own money, why would I need his?

INSPECTOR SANSCLOU. Monsieur Har-harp—Harpagon, does he speak the truth?

HARPAGON. Yes, he's a well-respected man in the neighborhood. He's never been here before.

INSPECTOR SANSCLOU. *(to* **ANSELME***)* Quite right. I was just testing you, monsieur. *(to the group of suspects)* By the process of elimination, I now know who the brigand thief is. I have eliminated…the women, because they are stupid, frail, ignorant creatures with soft hearts—except for whores, of course—and would simply not have the courage to steal a man's cashbox from under his eyes. Obviously you, monsieur Har-harp-Harpagon, would not have a motive to steal your own cashbox, so you are eliminated. Maitre Jacques, the cook—

MAITRE JACQUES. Ze chef. I am ze chef!

INSPECTOR SANSCLOU. Yes, ze chef, you love to cook more than anything in the world, and would never leave your kitchen, your coq au vin and especially a rising soufflé to steal a cashbox, so you are eliminated.

(pointing to **LA FLECHE**, *who is now virtually drooling like the village idiot)*

INSPECTOR SANSCLOU. *(cont.)* We can certainly eliminate him...

(to **CLEANTE***)*

I was sorely tempted to name you, the son and heir to the fortune, but I don't think you would do such a thing in the middle of a courtship of a beautiful young lady. What kind of impression would that make!? So that leaves...your enigmatic valet, Valere, who has no past, and arrived on your doorstep seemingly on a "wave" of mystery. You know nothing about him except this alleged shipwreck—

ELISE. It was a real shipwreck! I was there! He could not have done it!

INSPECTOR SANSCLOU. Testimony from a loved one is inadmissible. *(to* **VALERE***)* And of course, the most damning piece of evidence, you are a servant.

VALERE. It happens I am not a servant. And if you knew who I really was, you would tremble at accusing me of this crime.

INSPECTOR SANSCLOU. If you are not a servant, why are you dressed like one? Why do you work like one?

VALERE. I have been traveling incognito, searching for my long lost relatives.

INSPECTOR SANSCLOU. *(writing)* I-N-C-O-G...

VALERE. –N—I—T—O.

INSPECTOR SANSCLOU. I knew that. And where are these relatives?

VALERE. If any of them are still alive, they will be in Spain.

ANSELME. Spain!?

VALERE. Near Barthelona.

ANSELME. Barthelona!? Be careful what you fabricate, young man, I am well acquainted with the region around Barthelona.

VALERE. Then you have no doubt heard of San Burgos de La Extremadura Cathtella Villa Nueva del Cordoba Tacarimba de Almadóvar.

ANSELME. Heard of it? I'm from there!

VALERE. Then you have no doubt heard of Don Fernando de Valenzuela.

ANSELME. It happens that no one could know him better than I.

VALERE. Well, that is the man, were he still alive, who would attest to my noble heritage, since it is he who gave me life.

ANSELME. Impossible! *(to* **INSPECTOR SANSCLOU***)* Arrest him. He is an imposter! The son of Don Fernando de Valenzuela died in a shipwreck sixteen years ago, along with his sister and mother, as they were fleeing civil unrest in San Burgos de La Extremadura Cathtella Villa Nueva del Cordoba Tacarimba de Almadóvar.

VALERE. Just a moment! That son, age seven, was saved from the shipwreck.

(with a gasp, everyone gathers around **VALERE***)*

I will tell you a story, so unbelievable in its horror and triumph, that you will think me a fabricator of tales. But every word is true. That young boy was standing with the captain on the poop when a sudden squall came up. The ship was tossed against a rock when it was thrown off course…

(the group jerks)

And the young lad and the captain were thrown into the churning waters.

ALL. OH!

VALERE. But the captain, a very seaworthy man, held onto the lad, grabbed a rock protruding from the black, choppy waters, lifted the lad up on it and together they watched while the ship was torn into pieces and went down. That lad was…myself.

ALL. OH!

VALERE. Seeing that the poor child had lost everything, the captain, a noble Spanish sailor, with no children of his own, took me under his wing, brought me up, educated me, and trained me in the profession of soldiering ever since I was old enough to learn. I was in Italy when I heard news that perhaps my father had not drowned in the shipwreck, and I hopped on a vessel to travel back to Spain.

ALL. *(happy)* Ah!

VALERE. It was on that ship that I met the beautiful, charming, heavenly Elise, and on that same ship that I experienced another dreadful shipwreck.

ALL. No!

LA FLECHE. I think you should avoid all sea travel in the future.

VALERE. Good idea. Nevertheless, this was a most fortunate shipwreck, as she reciprocated my tender passion and we fell in love. I resolved to stop here, to be near her, and I sent my trusted servant Pedro to discover my father's whereabouts. I took a position myself as a servant to her father, having lost all my money in the second shipwreck. I am now awaiting news from Pedro.

INSPECTOR SANSCLOU. This is all rather preposterous, you realize.

HARPAGON. Preposterous!

ANSELME. What proof do you have that any of this is true?

VALERE. The Spanish Captain, Bernardo Alba del Lope de Vega Garcia Lorca, now retired, who lives in La Battagliola de Lambrusco Grasparossa del Fuego, will tell you the story. And I have this ring that belonged to my mother.

ANSELME. *(looking at the ring)* Impossible!

MARIANNE. *(looking at the ring)* Impossible!

VALERE. Why?

MARIANNE. I must tell you an equally amazing story.

(as everyone gathers around her)

MARIANNE.*(cont.)* My poor, frail, invalid mother has recounted our tale of woe so many times that I can relate it almost word for word. I was a small child of four, so I have little memory of the experience of being thrown from the deck of a ship—

(larger jerk from the crowd)

– into the water, grabbing onto a piece of the hull with my mother, cruelly tossed about in the cold, unrepentant sea…she tells me it was many days before we were spotted by…a pirate ship!

ALL. OH!

MARIANNE. They had decided to turn us into slaves, but the captain developed a soft spot in his heart for me, so my mother became the ship's laundress and I became the darling of the pirates. A sort of good luck charm. I grew up on that ship, standing at the point of the bow, watching the waves rise and fall, fall and rise…

(The group sways with more vigor.)

Until the pirate ship was captured and we were put down in the port of Naples, with nothing but our meager possessions.

ALL. Awww.

MARIANNE. We discovered, in Naples, that my mother had been deprived of all her property by some mercenary distant relatives, and there was no news of my father or my brother. My mother, heartbroken, had a small inheritance from her family, and we went to retrieve it in Genoa and then we moved here. But the rigors of being a pirate laundress were too much for her, so she is as you shortly will see her—poor, frail and invalid.

ALL. *(weeping and sniffing, except* **HARPAGON***)* DREADFUL!

MARIANNE. All I have left of my childhood is this ring. My mother had one made for my brother and one for me in the exact image of her own!

*(**MARIANNE** holds out her hand, **VALERE** holds out his hand, and they compare rings.)*

MARIANNE. *(cont.)* My brother!

VALERE. My sister!

ANSELME. My children!

ALL. WHAT!?

HARPAGON. What's happening here?!

ANSELME. *(as they gather around* **ANSELME***)* Yes, you're my daughter, and you're my son! I am Don Fernando de Valenzuela, whom Heaven saved from the waves of that dreadful shipwreck. As though it were yesterday, I remember standing on the deck, watching the crew fight the storm as their oars dipped and pulled, pulled and dipped—

(very vigorous motions from the group)

But, alas, the relentless tempest proved too much for the captain and the crew and we were all thrown into the raging sea. As luck would have it, I had all my fortune with me in waterproof bags—pig bladder, I think they were—but what did that mean to me when my children and my wife had been lost? All these years, I believed you had perished in that storm. The pain of the loss was too great to bear and I changed my name and traveled here, to try and forget...

(copious weeping from everyone except **HARPAGON***, over music)*

Although sometimes, on dark, lonely nights, I still dared to dream that someday I might find them. At last, just a week ago, the loneliness overcame me, and I decided to take a wife, someone kind and gentle to be my companion. And now, God be praised, I have regained my family!

(He embraces his children, they embrace him and each other, everyone pulls out handkerchiefs and blows their noses, except **HARPAGON.***)*

HARPAGON. Now let me get this straight. You're his daughter?

MARIANNE. *(pointing to* **HARPAGON***)* I am! Do I have to marry him, father?

ANSELME. Not if you don't want to.

HARPAGON. *(to* **VALERE***)* And you are his son?

VALERE. I am. And by the way, I quit. *(bringing* **ELISE** *to his father)* Father, this is the beautiful, intelligent, kind young woman I wish to take as a bride.

ANSELME. Do you love her?

VALERE. With every fiber of my being.

ANSELME. You have my consent.

HARPAGON. She has no dowry!

ANSELME. I have plenty of money for a dowry.

ELISE. Heaven bless pig bladder!

MARIANNE. *(bringing* **CLEANTE** *to her father)* Father, this is the man I wish to marry. May I?

ANSELME. *(to* **CLEANTE***)* Young man, do you love her? Are you an honest man?

CLEANTE. Yes and yes.

ANSELME. Then there is nothing more to say!

HARPAGON. Oh yes there is! I still don't have my cashbox!

INSPECTOR SANSCLOU. Very true, and let me say, family reunion notwithstanding, that your son is the prime suspect.

ANSELME. You are mistaken. No one in the family of Fernando de Valenzuela from San Burgos de La Extremadura Cathtella Villa Nueva del Cordoba Tacarimba de Almadóvar near Barthelona has ever been or ever will be a thief.

HARPAGON. Well, somebody took the cashbox! And I am missing fifty thousand in gold, and until my money is retrieved, neither of my children has permission to marry anybody! And no one is to leave this room!

LA FLECHE. I think I can clear up this matter.

INSPECTOR SANSCLOU. You!? You're an idiot!

HARPAGON. I always said he was. But a shrewd idiot.

LA FLECHE Not so much an idiot that I can't solve the mystery of the missing cashbox.

*(***MARIANNE**, **CLEANTE**, **ELISE**, *and* **VALERE** *look at him with terror in their eyes.)*

LA FLECHE. *(cont.)* It's quite simple, as I'm sure Inspector Sansclou will agree. And, in fact, I tracked the thief and retrieved your cashbox, with its contents...mostly intact.

(They all lean in, breathlessly expectant.)

It was Maitre Simon in the garden with the shovel.

(The four lovers breathe a sigh of relief.)

INSPECTOR SANSCLOU. How do you know that, monsieur?

LA FLECHE. I saw him digging?

HARPAGON. What do you mean, mostly intact?

LA FLECHE. Maitre Simon extracted his fee, which he had not yet received from you.

HARPAGON. I was going to pay him—in time!

LA FLECHE. Well, the time had come. I followed him and convinced him to return the box to me.

HARPAGON. Oh all right, all right! Where's my cashbox? Where is it!?

LA FLECHE. I have it in custody, and you'll receive it the moment you consent to the two marriages of your children, and pay for the weddings. Big ones, in the big church downtown. With a reception, and Maitre Jacques preparing the banquet.

MAITRE JACQUES. *(grabbing the pen at the desk and writing)* We'll start with canapés...a wonderful Perrier-Jouet 47...

HARPAGON. That'll cost a fortune!

LA FLECHE. Nowhere near as much as the fifty thousand you're currently missing.

HARPAGON. That's blackmail! Arrest him, Sansclou!

(Everyone looks at him, trembling. A pause while he considers.)

INSPECTOR SANSCLOU. I don't think so.

ANSELME. Give him his money. I'll pay for both weddings AND the banquet.

MARIANNE & VALERE. Oh father!

LA FLECHE. No, monsieur. We are dealing with principle, and a very important lesson. Aren't we, Mme. Poquelin?

FROSINE. *(removing her warts, wig, and the nose and speaking in her normal voice)* We are indeed.

HARPAGON. Oh, you look so much better!

FROSINE. *(flirting)* Thank you.

LA FLECHE. Your fortune will be returned when you promise, on your sacred oath, on the grave of your late wife, whom you probably put there due to your miserly behavior, that you will reform. That you will bestow wedding presents upon your children, that you will feed your horses until their ribs disappear and they are smiling, and you will pay your servants a fair wage—with retirement benefits—*and* dental, and buy yourself a brand new suit of clothes for the wedding.

HARPAGON. *(going to his desk and adding it up)* But that'll cost me—

LA FLECHE. Ah, ah, ah! No promise, no cashbox.

HARPAGON. All right, all right! I promise.

ELISE & CLEANTE. Oh father!

(They kiss him on either cheek. He grimaces, then smiles.)

HARPAGON. Well, where is it?

*(**LA FLECHE** nods to **MARIANNE**, who hops over to him. He lifts her skirt and retrieves the cashbox from underneath her copious skirts.)*

Oh, my cashbox, my blessed cashbox!

(Now he cries like a baby.)

MAITRE JACQUES. Oh, la, la, I must go and check on ze soufflé and ze coq au vin!

(He exits.)

MARIANNE. I must go tell my mother!

ANSELME. I must go and rejoin my wife!

CLEANTE. I must go meet my future mother-in-law!

(They all three exit.)

INSPECTOR SANSCLOU. I must go and make my report!

(He exits.)

ELISE. I must set the table for dinner!

VALERE. I'll help you!

(The two of them exit.)

FROSINE. And I must compare fortunes with this charming, handsome man!

(She opens her cashbox. He opens his. They compare weights, laugh, flirt, and he starts for the garden, she following. Just before she exits, she turns to the audience, opens the box, takes out a coin, unwraps it and places the chocolate in her mouth.)

Of course they're fake!

(She exits into the garden. We see dirt being thrown up. **LA FLECHE** *is alone on stage.)*

LA FLECHE. And thereby hangs a tale of money lost
And love regained at clever, comic cost.
All right, it isn't Lear, but in these times,
These dire, woeful economic climes,
'Tis pity not to smile and be lighthearted.
So now we end what we heretofore started,
You'll leave this theatre, just a little wiser,
And never will you dare to be a miser!

(Music. **LA FLECHE** *exits, and curtain calls commence.)*

THE END

Also by
Freyda Thomas...

The Learned Ladies

Tartuffe: Born Again

50 Fabulous Classical Monologues For Men

(with Jan Silverman)

50 Fabulous Classical Monologues For Women

(with Jan Silverman)

Please visit our website **samuelfrench.com** for complete descriptions and licensing information.

OTHER TITLES AVAILABLE FROM SAMUEL FRENCH

THE LEARNED LADIES

Molière
Translated and Adapted by Freyda Thomas

Farce / 5m, 6f (doubling possible) / Interior

This rollicking version of *Les Femmes Savantes* delighted audiences Off Broadway in a production starring Jean Stapleton as Philamente, a most unliterary lady intent on having a high toned literary salon. She has neither literary nor common sense, which makes her easy prey for sycophantic con artist Trissotin. He passes himself off as a famous poet and becomes a permanent house guest. Philamente hopes to marry her daughter to Trissotin, but the daughter wishes to marry the unsuitable Clitandre. This version strays from a strictly literal translation of Moliere's play, often employing anachronisms in the rhymed couplets that will appall purists and absolutely delight everyone else. If you want your audiences to roll with laughter as they watch a play by a "famous dead playwright," this version is for you.

"Thomas' modernisms smartly put the satire's emphasis on the pomposity rather than the feminism of the Précieuse Movement."
– *Variety*

SAMUELFRENCH.COM

OTHER TITLES AVAILABLE FROM SAMUEL FRENCH

TARTUFFE: BORN AGAIN

Molière
Translated and Adapted by Freyda Thomas

Farce / 6m, 5f / Interior

This modern adaptation casts Tartuffe as a deposed televangelist who rooks Orgon and his family of their money and property and nearly compromises Orgon's wife. The action takes place in a religious television studio in Baton Rouge where the characters cavort to either prevent or aid Tartuffe in his machinations. Written in modern verse, *Tartuffe: Born Again* adheres closely to the structure and form of the original. Moliere's legendary comedic characters are delightfully at home in this modern day version that played at New York's Circle in the Square.

SAMUELFRENCH.COM

www.ingramcontent.com/pod-product-compliance
Lightning Source LLC
Chambersburg PA
CBHW071410290426
44108CB00014B/1766